PERIYAR

PERIYAR

A POLITICAL BIOGRAPHY OF E.V. RAMASAMY

BALA JEYARAMAN

RAINLIGHT
RUPA

Published in RAINLIGHT by
Rupa Publications India Pvt. Ltd 2013
7/16, Ansari Road, Daryaganj
New Delhi 110002

Sales centres:
Allahabad Bengaluru Chennai
Hyderabad Jaipur Kathmandu
Kolkata Mumbai

Copyright © Bala Jeyaraman 2013

Published in association with New Horizon Media, Chennai.

All rights reserved.
No part of this publication may be reproduced, transmitted,
or stored in a retrieval system, in any form or by any means,
electronic, mechanical, photocopying, recording or otherwise,
without the prior permission of the publisher.

ISBN: 978-81-291-2385-5

10 9 8 7 6 5 4 3 2 1

The moral right of the author has been asserted.

This book is sold subject to the condition that it shall not,
by way of trade or otherwise, be lent, resold, hired out, or otherwise
circulated, without the publisher's prior consent, in any form of binding or
cover other than that in which it is published.

Contents

Preface   *vii*

1   The Early Years   1
2   In the Congress   10
3   A Radical Agenda   20
4   Flirting with Socialism   28
5   The Language War   36
6   Promised Lands   44
7   The Big Split   54
8   Strangers in a Strange Republic   66
9   An Uneasy Alliance   76
10   Enemies to Friends   87
11   The Legacy   98

Timeline   105
Endnotes   109
References   122

Preface

I owe my interest in the Dravidian movement to my maternal grandfather and namesake. From the time he was denied a scholarship at school because of his caste in the late 1930s, till his death in 2006, the man was a hardcore Dravidian enthusiast. He was a good example of some of the contradictions that characterize the movement's ordinary supporters—he liked Periyar's message of social reform but voted for DMK all his life; he would rant against Brahminism and caste discrimination, but zealously safeguard his own caste identity at the same time; he accepted Periyar's Dravidian racial hypothesis but not his views on women's emancipation.

I grew up reading official hagiographies of Periyar. Without exception, they were full of admiration for the man and his ideals. An unbiased observer would be compelled to believe that he was nothing short of a superman who abolished caste, eradicated superstitions and liberated women all by himself. Every Tamil book I read about Periyar was full of anecdotes and vignettes that sought to establish his greatness. Not a single word of dissent could be found in my textbooks. However, later from the discussion boards and forum threads on the

Internet, I discovered that there were also people who were antipathic towards him.

Periyar's life and actions provoke extreme reactions from people and it is difficult to write a balanced biography of the man. He is neither the superman his admirers make him out to be nor the hateful demagogue his opponents say he was. He was an extraordinary man who had a long and eventful life. He was an integral part of much of the history of twentieth century Tamil Nadu. In this book, I have tried to depict his actions in the context of the larger picture.

Many biographies (and the mediocre 2007 film on him) talk about his early years disproportionately and tend to skim over his later life. But I have dedicated only one chapter to cover his life till he joined the Indian National Congress in 1918. I have generally avoided anecdotes and vignettes and recounted the major events in Periyar's life in a chronologically linear presentation, in the context of events in the outside world. But for the last chapter, it concentrates on events in Periyar's life and does not attempt to analyze his policies. I have used footnotes to prevent certain explanations from impending the flow of the narrative.

R. Kannan's exhaustive biography of C.N. Annadurai served as a model for writing this book. It proved to me that it is possible to write a dispassionate and engaging biography of a larger-than-life personality without succumbing to rhetoric and hyperbole. My experience with English Wikipedia gave me a healthy skepticism for primary accounts and using a single source. Except for the early years of Periyar's life (for which a biographer is forced to depend on Sami Chidambaram's account and Periyar's own words), I have attempted to source the rest of the book from secondary sources and newspaper accounts. Any factual errors present in this book are due to my inability to verify those accounts.

Periyar is referred to by many names. His full name at birth was Erode Venkatappa Ramasamy Naicker. He dropped the caste suffix 'Naicker' in 1929. The title 'Periyar' was given to him in 1938 and it stuck. His followers call him 'Thanthai Periyar' (father Periyar), while his opponents mostly avoid the 'Periyar' title and call him by his initials (as EVR or EeVeRa) or use his caste suffix intentionally. I have used the name 'Periyar' throughout the book for the sake of uniformity. Wherever the word 'state' is used in the book, it refers to either the Madras Presidency—a province of British India till 1947 or its successor in the republic of India—the Madras State (renamed Tamil Nadu in 1969). The term 'government' is usually used with qualifiers like the 'Rajaji government' or the 'colonial government'. Keeping the non-Tamil reader in mind, I have used equivalent English terms in most places while providing the relevant Tamil terms either in italics or within parentheses.

Finally, I wish to thank my mother Poongothai for encouraging me to accept the offer to write this book and my fellow Wikipedians for showing me the value of research.

Bala Jeyaraman
September 2010, Coimbatore

1
The Early Years

I talked with my rustic customers and fellow merchants. I also spoke with the pious devotees and priests. These conversations generally gave shape to my anti-religion, anti-shastra, anti-purana and atheist policies. They formed the basis for my views on caste, God and religion. I also developed a general distaste for Brahminism.

—Periyar, on his childhood days (XX: p5)

The boy was shackled and chained to a log. He had been beating up his classmates again. Tired of the complaints from his teacher, the boy's father had him confined at home and tied to a log too heavy for him; or so his father thought. Once his father's back was turned, the boy lifted the log on his shoulders and ran away to join his friends together with the shackles and chain. The incident with the log was a portent of things to come later in his life. Time and again, his opponents, who smugly assumed they had cornered or defeated him, would be foxed to find him bouncing back stronger than before. The boy's name was Ramasamy. Years later, he would come to be known as Periyar (the great elder).

His Family

Periyar was born at Erode on 17 September 1879. His family was a Kannada Balija Naidu family that had settled in Erode. His father, Venkatar Naicker, was a wealthy merchant—a self-made man who had started his life as a labourer in a stone quarry.

Venkatar and his wife, Chinnathai, had been childless for ten years into their marriage. They had visited many temples and prayed to many deities asking for a child. Their piety had grown and finally they became devotees of Lord Venkatachalapathi (Vishnu) of Tirupati. So, when their boys were born, they named them Krishnasamy and Ramasamy after the avataras of Vishnu.

Krishnasamy was two years elder to Ramasamy. The two boys had two younger sisters—Ponnuthai and Kannamma. All four children were brought up in comfort by Venkatar. Krishnasamy was the calmer of the two boys—he was obedient and soft-spoken. Ramasamy, in complete contrast, was full of questions and mischief. Even before he was five, his exploits had become widely known in the neighbourhood.

His Childhood

Periyar's comfortable life came to an end when he was five years old. His father abruptly gave him up in adoption to his grand aunt. The old woman had lost her husband and needed a male to run the household after her. Since Venkatar had two sons, she asked him to give her one of them. When Periyar heard the news, he thought 'adoption' was some kind of a sweet snack.

Periyar's grand aunt was a poor woman. On some days, he even had to go to bed hungry. But poverty did not dent his penchant for mischief; his days were spent pulling pranks on his neighbours. He was very inquisitive—he would pester guests with questions till they were tired of him. His foster mother decided to send him to school to put an end to his mischief. School did not reform Periyar, instead, it offered him plenty of new opportunities to learn new tricks. It was a veranda school where fifty boys spent their days cooped up in close proximity. Soon, he was getting into fist fights with his classmates.

Periyar first encountered casteism at school. His parents observed caste rituals strictly and forbade him from touching people of certain other castes. If he did so, he had to bathe immediately to get rid of the 'taint'. All his fellow students would drink water only from the house of their teacher—an upper caste Shaiva (Shiva worshipper). But he would eye the houses of Vaniya Chettis, bamboo weavers and Muslims, on his way to school. He wondered why his parents wouldn't let him drink water from their houses. 'Maybe their drinking water tastes bitter,' he thought.

One day, he drank water at a Chettiar's house, impressing his friends with his act of bravado. Soon he was having snacks at the Chettiar's house. This was the last straw for Venkatar—he withdrew Periyar from the school. But stopping the boy from going to school was not easy—even chaining him at home did not work. Finally, Venkatar took him back from his foster mother and asked him to accompany him to the mandi (godown) instead.

His Marriage

Periyar was happy at the godown. He started as an errand boy, shouting out the prices of commodities and writing addresses on parcels. He soon learnt all the aspects of his father's business and started managing the godown. He made a lot of friends in the market due to his ready wit. When the crowds thinned after the morning rush, the neighbouring traders would come over to his shop to hear him talk. He used his razor sharp tongue to make fun of pious and religious people. The priests and astrologers who frequented his house would instantly leave the place when he was around, in fear of having to answer his incisive questions. His fame as a debater and an outspoken atheist grew in the market.

As he grew into his teens, his circle of friends became wider. He would organize lavish parties for his friends on the river bank every night. His parents, worried by his philandering, decided to get him married. As Venkatar was a very rich merchant, marriage alliances from rich landlords and merchants were aplenty. But Periyar had already chosen his bride—his distant relative Nagammal. A few years younger than him, she was a shy girl whom he had first met at a relative's wedding. But she was not considered a proper match for him as her father was not wealthy. However, knowing their son's obstinate mind, Venkatar and Chinnathai approved the match.

Chinnathai had hoped that her new daughter-in-law would change the rebellious ways of her son. But, instead, Periyar's influence on Nagammal proved stronger. He even made her remove her thali—the sacred yellow thread worn by married Tamil women.

Periyar and Nagammal did not have any children even after a few years of marriage. At Chinnathai's insistence, Nagammal began praying at the local temple for a child. At first, Periyar did not mind, but he became extremely annoyed when she started spending more and more time at the temple. He decided to teach her a lesson.

One day, Nagammal was waylaid by four rowdies on her way to the temple. They teased her mercilessly and she ran home crying. Periyar consoled her saying even temples were not safe for her. The whole thing had been his plan—he had arranged for his friends to harangue her to prove that gods cannot help people.

After five years of marriage, Nagammal finally became pregnant. But the couple's happiness was cut short when their baby died soon after birth. Periyar sank into despair and found solace in courtesans. When Venkatar publicly rebuked him for treating his wife badly, he became angry and ran away from home. He was twenty-five at that time.

A Runaway at Kashi (Varanasi)

Periyar's first stop was at Bezawada (Vijayawada) in Andhra Pradesh. Though he was wearing several jewels, he could not bring himself to pawn them. Instead, he begged in the streets for food. He befriended two Brahmins—Ganapathi Iyer and Venkataramana Iyer, who were planning to go to Kashi. They convinced him to come along by describing it as a place of plenty where there was no shortage of food for anyone.

They reached Hyderabad first and supported themselves there by begging. They slept at an inn meant for pilgrims at night and begged during the day. In the evenings, they would discuss Hindu shastras (laws) and puranas (epics) to while away their free time. The two Brahmins, who were staunch believers, became targets for Periyar's ridicule. He would question them about shastras and make fun of the Ramayana and the Mahabharata.

Crowds began to gather at the inn to hear the three argue. They soon turned it into a three man act and started performing at weddings and other functions. They befriended a government official—Murugesa Mudaliar, who let them stay in his house. When they later left for Kashi, Mudaliar gave Periyar a hundred rupees for his expenses, and Periyar left his jewels in Mudaliar's care.

Once the travellers reached Kashi, Periyar's two Brahmin friends left him to his own devices and went their own way. He soon found that the actual Kashi bore little resemblance to what he had imagined, based on their description. After his last paisa was used up, finding food became tough. There were maths (monasteries) that fed beggars. But when he tried to enter one, he was thrown out as he was not a Brahmin.

Overcome with hunger, he scavenged for leftovers in the garbage. He met the same reaction in all the monasteries—they would not let a non-Brahmin in. He came up with a plan to get food regularly—passing himself off as a Brahmin. He shaved off his beard and moustache and started wearing a poonool (sacred thread worn by Brahmins).

The next monastery he approached let him in. They offered him a meal a day in turn for picking leaves from vilva trees. The job was difficult—he had to get up at five in the morning, have a dip in the Ganga and return with the leaves by five-thirty. Then he had to light all the lamps. But it was the bathing that was the toughest for him. He was not accustomed to bathing in cold water early in the morning chill. Therefore, instead of taking a bath, he started just wetting himself with a damp towel. But he was soon caught in the act and thrown out of the monastery. He went back to begging along the riverbank.

There was a large crowd of beggars there dependent on the charity of pilgrims who came to Kashi for the funeral rites of their relatives.

After a few days, Periyar noticed a female beggar selling herself for food. This opened his eyes and he began taking a closer look at his surroundings. He found that the priests cheated the pilgrims of their money—they would not complete the ritual incantations and had no regard for religious propriety. They sold overpriced remedies for sins and indulged in other unlawful activities. Periyar's experiences in Kashi left a deep impression on him and affected how he viewed Brahmins thereafter. He had already seen how Brahmins in his home town were treated preferentially.[1] Kashi strengthened his aversion to them. He had had enough of the place and decided to return home.

The Businessman

Periyar did not return home directly. He did not wish to face his father. Instead, he went to the house of Subramania Pillai in Ellur (currently in Kerala). Pillai was a government official and an old friend of Venkatar. He fed and housed Periyar. At Periyar's request, he did not inform Venkatar that his son had returned. But after a few weeks, news reached Venkatar that his son was at Pillai's house. Venkatar rushed to Ellur and convinced Periyar to return home.

To keep his son occupied and happy, Venkatar gave him the full responsibility of running the family business. Periyar returned to work at the godown. He renewed his friendship with the neighbouring merchants. He also began to help people out in many ways. Invited or not, he would show up at all functions in the town and pitch in.

Periyar had a knack for administration and soon earned respect for his business acumen. Though he lacked formal education, he had a thorough knowledge of the law and its loopholes. His reputation for being level-headed and fair soon made him the unofficial arbiter of disputes amongst his fellow merchants. Whenever a dispute was brought to him to be judged, he always tried to reach a compromise first. He also involved himself in public activities. He gained a reputation for getting things done. If the people wanted roads for their town, they went to Periyar. If they wanted to conduct a function in a temple, they called on him. He spent much of his time talking to businessmen, government officials, landlords and local bigwigs. In 1905, plague hit Erode and its surrounding areas, and Periyar was at the forefront of the relief measures. He and his friends helped get the afflicted people to hospitals. He paid for their treatment and even carried the dead on his own shoulders for burial. In 1910, Periyar officially became a member of the Erode Municipal Council.

Apart from his council post, he was also the chairman of the Erode Devasthanam (temple board). Though he was a staunch atheist and believed spending money on temples was a waste of public resources, he performed his duties admirably. He did not let his personal feelings come in the way of running the board. He was mindful of the people's sentiments and abided by them. The board was running deficits when he took over. Within a year of his skilful administration, it showed a surplus of forty-five thousand rupees. Due to these successes, he became the chairman of the Municipal Council in 1918.

One of his major accomplishments as chairman was solving the problem of scarcity of drinking water in the town. He found out which government departments and officials dealt with the issue and wrote to them asking for a proper drinking water supply system. His persistent efforts paid off and soon, Erode had an excellent water supply system installed. The functioning of the public sanitation department under him was so efficient that the neighbouring Salem Municipal Council asked him to depute his officials to their town. As chairman, Periyar was unafraid and scrupulously honest. He did not allow past associations or friendships to intervene when it came to safeguarding public interest. He defied his own merchant associates when he demolished their buildings to expand the Erode market in 1918.

Periyar's stint in the Municipal Council brought him to the attention of Indian National Congress leaders of the Madras Presidency. The Congressmen were then in the midst of a tussle with the Justice Party to win over the non-Brahmins of the province. They recruited Periyar for their cause. Thus began his association with the Congress party.

2
In the Congress

> *President sir, I have lost hope that non-Brahmins will get any justice from the Congress party. I am walking out of the party this very minute. Hereafter, it will be my primary goal to destroy the Congress which protects caste and Varnashrama.*
> —Periyar announcing his resignation from the Congress at the Kanchipuram conference. November 1925 (XXII: p62)

Birth of Justice Party

The Indian National Congress' rank and file was dominated by Brahmin members. The Brahmins also occupied a majority of government posts and controlled the selection of candidates to the provincial legislature. This caused resentment among the non-Brahmin sections of the political class.

There were three Brahmin factions within the Congress—

the Mylapore and Egmore factions which favoured contesting elections and working from within the system, and the more militant Salem nationalists who did not want to cooperate with the British. The Mylapore faction comprised Chetpet Iyers and Vembakkam Iyengars. The Egmore faction was controlled by Kasturi Ranga Iyengar—the then editor of *The Hindu*. The 'no-changers' were led by C. Rajagopalachari.

Non-Brahmin leaders who did not get along with these factions routinely faced defeat in the elections. They decided to organize a non-Brahmin political alternative to the Congress. After a few unsuccessful attempts, the South Indian Liberal Federation was formed in 1916 by Dr T.M. Nair and P. Theagaraya Chetty to represent non-Brahmin interests. Both men wielded enormous influence on the non-Brahmins and bore a grudge against the Brahmin factions for defeating them in previous elections. Their party came be to popularly known as the Justice Party after the English newspaper, *Justice,* published by it.

Within a few years of its foundation, the Justice Party garnered support from the non-Brahmins as well as some sections of the colonial bureaucracy. The non-Brahmins saw it as an opportunity to achieve political power on their own and the British administrators viewed it as a way to check the growth of nationalism in the province.

In 1917, the British announced their intention to introduce political reforms in India. The Montagu-Chelmsford committee was formed to hear representations from various sections of Indian people on their views on political reform. The Justice Party made a vociferous demand for communal representation for the non-Brahmins in the new political system, similar to the one granted to the Muslims in 1909. They asked for caste-based reservation of seats in the new legislature with separate electorates.

The Congress was alarmed at the growing support for the Justice Party. To compete with them, it decided to organize its own non-Brahmin faction.

The Madras Presidency Association

The Congress began looking for non-Brahmin leaders who could effectively counter the Justice Party charge against Brahmin domination in the party. The Madras Presidency Association (MPA) was formed under Gooty Kesava Pillai and started recruiting popular non-Brahmin leaders to represent it. Periyar was then a member of the Erode Municipal Council and a rising star in Erode district politics. He was recruited by the Congress along with Thiru V. Kalyanasundara Mudaliar (Thiru Vi Ka) and P. Varadarajulu Naidu, to represent the non-Brahmins within the party.

Montagu, the then Secretary of State for India, visited the country to hear the views of various Indian groups about the proposed political reforms. The MPA held its first meeting in September 1917 and decided to send a representation to meet Montagu. It was an attempt to demonstrate that the Justice Party alone did not speak for all non-Brahmins in the province. Periyar was elected as one of the vice-presidents of the MPA. It was his first formal association with a Congress organization. He had a high opinion of the party's nationalistic ideals and believed it could bring about social reform. But the MPA was doomed from the start due to opposition from the Brahmin Congress members. They were opposed to any form of communal representation or separate electorates.

In order to compete with the Justice Party as representatives of non-Brahmins, and counter their charges of being puppets of Brahmins, the MPA was forced to adopt an agenda similar to the Justice programme. This was not acceptable to the Congress which disassociated itself from the MPA. Besides organizing a few public meetings and publishing periodicals like *Indian Patriot* and *Desabhaktan*, the MPA got nowhere politically and was eventually wound up in 1920. A frustrated Kesava Pillai joined the Justice Party but Periyar stayed with the Congress. When reforms eventually happened, communal representation was given for non-Brahmins but there were no separate electorates for them.

Periyar in the Congress

During his time in the MPA, Periyar grew closer to the Congress leaders and joined the Congress formally in 1919. He had become the chairman of the Erode Municipal Council the previous year and this had brought him in close contact with the Congress chairman of the Municipal Council of the neighbouring town of Salem—a lawyer named C. Rajagopalachari. Popularly called Rajaji, he was the leader of the 'no cooperation with British' faction of the Congress.

Rajaji recognized the potential of the dynamic Erode chairman—the Congress needed popular non-Brahmin leaders. He began meeting Periyar whenever he came to Erode. The two men soon became friends and would discuss various political and social issues. Varadarajulu Naidu, another Congress leader from Salem, also met Periyar often.

Naidu and Rajaji convinced Periyar to join the Congress. The party's professed ideals—nationalism, emancipation of the oppressed classes, social reform and prohibition—appealed to the reform-minded Periyar. He believed he would be able to achieve communal representation through the party. His high regard for Mahatma Gandhi was also an important factor in his joining the Congress.

In 1920, the Congress, dissatisfied by the insignificant extent of political reforms and outraged by the Jallianwala Bagh massacre, launched the Non-Cooperation Movement. All Congress members resigned from their posts and joined the agitation. Periyar was then holding twenty-nine official and nominated posts[2] in Erode. He resigned from all of them, including his chairmanship of the Erode Municipal Council, and plunged headlong into the nationalist struggle. He adopted the khaddar[3] promotion programme of the Congress wholeheartedly. To Nagammal's surprise, he donated all the silk and foreign-made clothes in the house to the drama troupe of TKS Brothers to be used as costumes. He and his family members began wearing only khadi clothes.

Periyar not only set a personal example, he also began selling khaddar in the streets. It was a strange sight—the wealthy merchant was going from door to door extolling the virtues of khadi and the need to help the local economy by promoting Indian weavers. He was an instant success. Khaddar sales soared wherever he went and he drew large crowds who came to hear his blunt and witty speeches. Soon, Congressmen from neighbouring towns kept him busy with requests to promote khaddar in their areas.

In November 1921, Mahatma Gandhi called for the boycott of toddy shops as part of the Non-Cooperation Movement. The prohibition agenda of the party was to be implemented by picketing toddy shops and other establishments that sold alcohol. In North India, palm trees were used to make toddy and they were cut down in some places as part of the prohibition agitation. In the southern parts of the country, toddy was extracted from palm and coconut trees.

Periyar himself owned a huge grove of five hundred coconut

trees. When he heard about palm trees being cut down in the north, he ordered his own coconut grove to be cut down. This act resulted in a loss of an annual revenue of fifty thousand rupees to him and sent shock waves through the Congress. Till then, the rich men in the party had led a cushy existence without suffering any personal loss. Not only did Periyar cut down his grove at a huge personal loss but also got himself arrested by personally picketing toddy shops. When he was in jail, Nagammal and his sister Kannamma took his place in the picket lines and carried on his work.

The Non-Cooperation Movement wound down after a couple of years. While the Congressmen were protesting in the streets, the Justice Party had contested the 1920 elections and formed the first government under the new diarchal[4] system of governance. By 1923, a sizeable section in the Congress regretted boycotting the legislature and wanted to participate in the electoral process. They split from the Congress and formed the Swaraj Party. The Swarajist faction was led by Rajaji's rival, S. Satyamurti[5] in the Madras Presidency. Periyar, however, stayed with the Rajaji faction.

The Hero of Vaikom

Periyar's reputation as an organizer soon thrust him into the forefront of the struggle against untouchability in Vaikom, a town in the princely state of Travancore ruled by the king, Moolam Thirunal. It was the site of a famous Shiva temple. In other parts of the state of Travancore, untouchables like Ezhavas were not allowed to enter temples. But in Vaikom, they were not even allowed to use the roads around the temple. The Congress organized an agitation against this discriminatory practice in 1924. The agitation was led by local Congress leaders like K.P. Kesava Menon, T.K. Madhavan and George Joseph and it had the support of the national leadership of the Congress.

The conservative administration of the state represented by the king and his diwan, T. Raghavaiah, adamantly opposed the move to allow untouchables to use the roads. They cracked down on the agitation and arrested all the leaders. With the organizers in prison, the leadership looked for someone else to maintain the momentum of the struggle. They wrote to Periyar and invited him to come and take over the leadership of the agitation.

Periyar arrived at Vaikom in April 1924 and took over from the imprisoned Congress leaders. He too was arrested immediately and put in jail for a month. Some orthodox Brahmins performed a Shatru Samhara Yagna (a ritual praying for the death of the enemy) to kill him. Ironically, it was the king, Moolam Thirunal, who died shortly after.

As part of a clemency proposal due to the king's death, Periyar was released from prison. He was arrested again almost immediately for organizing protests. This time, he was sentenced to six months in jail. His place was taken by Nagammal and sister Kannamma who, along with the wives of T.K. Madhavan and Govindan Channar, kept the agitation going throughout the month of May. For her participation in the agitation, Nagammal too, was imprisoned.

After Moolam Thirunal's death, his senior wife—Sethu Lakshmibhai—became the queen regent ruling on behalf of the minor king Chithira Thirunal. Soon, the agitation grew and attracted support from other communities like Sikhs, Muslims and Christians. An alarmed Gandhi wanted to keep the agitation an intra-Hindu affair and started negotiating with the queen regent. After prolonged negotiations, a compromise was reached in November 1925—the untouchables were allowed to use three of the four roads around the temple. For his involvement in the agitation, the Tamil Nadu Congress Committee hailed Periyar as the Vaikom Veerar (Hero of Vaikom).[6]

The Cheranmadevi Incident

Periyar and other non-Brahmin leaders in the Congress did not like the Brahmin dominance in the party. Almost all major party posts were occupied by the Brahmins and Brahmin leaders like Rajaji and Satyamurti displayed their nepotism by appointing Brahmins to various posts. Even though Rajaji was a close friend, Periyar openly criticized the appointment of K. Santhanam (a Brahmin) as the head of the khaddar board by Rajaji. For five years, Periyar continued to believe that the Congress could be reformed from within. In 1925, an incident occurred that first showed him the futility of attempting internal reforms in the Congress.

V.V.S. Iyer, a Brahmin Congress leader, was running a gurukulam (residential school) at Cheranmadevi in Tirunelveli district. The school was sponsored mostly by donations from non-Brahmins. The Congress party too had pledged a sum of ten thousand rupees to it, out of which half had already been disbursed. In January 1925, reports reached Periyar that Brahmins and non-Brahmins were being treated differently in the school. The non-Brahmins were forced to eat separately from the Brahmins and different utensils were used to cook for both groups.

Periyar, one of the secretaries of the Tamil Nadu Congress Committee (TNCC), was outraged. He began a campaign with Varadarajulu Naidu against the discriminatory practice. Periyar withheld the remainder of the Congress donation till the practice was discontinued. But V.V.S. Iyer used his Brahmin support and bypassed Periyar. He obtained the money through Santhanam. Periyar and Naidu hit back with an anti-Brahmin campaign within the party. Periyar wrote to the non-Brahmin sponsors of the school informing them of the discriminatory practices. Slowly, donations to the school started drying up.

In April 1925, both men forced an open confrontation with the Brahmin faction at the TNCC meeting at Trichy. The Brahmin faction led by Rajaji and T.S.S. Rajan resisted attempts to cut off party aid to the school. As a compromise, both groups passed a resolution which merely advised all organizations involved in the nationalist movement to end discrimination based on birth. Even that was too much to stomach for Rajaji, who resigned from the committee. But Periyar succeeded in forcing the resignation of V.V.S. Iyer from the school through pressure from the non-Brahmin donors. The failure to get the Congress to do anything concrete with regard to ending caste discrimination within the party opened the eyes of Periyar to the futility of staying with the Congress.

The Final Break

Periyar's final break with the Congress came in November 1925. It was the inevitable culmination of a six year long struggle. When Rajaji had asked Periyar to join the Congress, he had assured him that the party would eventually adopt communal representation as an official policy. But it was a promise he did not intend to keep. The Brahmins in the Congress were completely against caste-based reservations as it threatened their dominance.

In the next six years, Periyar attempted as many times to include the issue of communal representation on the party platform. Every year during the annual party conferences, he tried to pass the communal resolution and was thwarted by the Brahmins.[7] He came close to succeeding in 1922 at the Tirupur conference, but was shouted down while reading the already prepared resolution.

In 1925, Periyar prepared to make his last attempt. The Cheranmadevi incident showed him the importance of mobilizing non-Brahmin support. For doing this, he started the periodical *Kudi Arasu* (The Republic) in May 1925. He used it to spread awareness about the need for reservation for non-Brahmins. Breaking with the party, it even supported the Hindu Religious Endowments Act passed by the Justice government. The Congress party did not like the independent functioning of *Kudi Arasu*.

The 1925 annual conference of the Congress was scheduled for 21-22 November at Kanchipuram. On 3 November, *Kudi Arasu* carried an article by Periyar which gave an indication of the planned confrontation. In the article, he warned the non-Brahmin representatives of 'a treacherous and selfish class of persons who deceive the public'—an allusion to the Brahmin faction. In the conference, he submitted two resolutions—both proposing communal representation for non-Brahmins. Bowing to pressure from the Brahmin faction, the conference president, Thiru Vi Ka, prevented him from tabling the resolutions. A disillusioned Periyar walked out of the party vowing to destroy it completely. The Congress had lost its most effective non-Brahmin leader.

3
A Radical Agenda

> *When we started the Self-Respect Movement, we had five basic goals—to destroy God, religion, Gandhi, Congress and the Brahmin.*
>
> —Periyar, in his last public speech (XV: p151)

After walking out of the Congress in November 1925, Periyar did not join any other party immediately. He retained his membership of the party's khaddar promotion board for another month. He received feelers from both the Congress (to come back) and the Justice Party (to join them) but he did neither. A month later, he announced the formation of a new organization—the Self-Respect Movement (Suya Mariyadhai Iyakkam).

A New Beginning

The Self-Respect Movement was not a political but a social reform movement. Promoting rationalism (pagutharivu), and eradicating caste and superstition were its main goals. Periyar did not have any intention of participating in electoral politics. He started a whirlwind tour of the state to promote his new radical policies. He spoke in favour of communal representation and against Varnashrama dharma—division of Hindu society according to the occupation of the people.

Though Periyar did not overtly support the Justice Party in his speeches, his political positions were identical to that of the party and he also made use of the party's periodicals to publish his ideas. When the third election to the Madras Legislative Council was announced in November 1926, there was a general expectation that he would formally declare his support to the Justice Party. The party was in a bad shape after six continuous years in power. Anti-incumbency sentiments and rising nationalistic fervour among the people had increased the support for the Swarajists.

The Justice Party desperately needed a mass campaigner like Periyar. But to their disappointment, he refused to endorse them openly. Instead, he announced that he would support qualified non-Brahmin candidates in the election. To counter Periyar's charges of favouritism toward Brahmins in the Congress, the Swarajists were forced to field more non-Brahmin candidates than they had planned.

Justice Party lost the election and the Swarajists emerged as the single largest party. Due to their policy of non-participation in the governing process, the Swarajists refused to take power. Governor George Goschen then formed a ministry of independents under P. Subbarayan.[8]

In 1927, Periyar began the anti-Brahmin campaign, which would become his signature political position in the coming years. The Justice Party had been founded on the basis of 'non-Brahminism' to ensure that the benefits of education and government jobs reached non-Brahmins. It did not have any radical social agenda of its own. It was satisfied with obtaining power and sharing the spoils. Periyar's arrival in the non-Brahmin camp shook it up and soon changed it into a general anti-Brahmin camp. This was achieved by a series of non-Brahmin conferences jointly organized by the Self-Respect Movement and the Justice Party. Periyar's influence on the Justicites was on the rise.

Self-Respecters' agenda was radical for their times. They wanted to do away with all religious and caste differences and the rituals that originated from them. They wanted to establish a casteless, classless society where a man's birth would have no impact on his social status. They favoured equal rights for women, widow remarriage, inter-caste and inter-religious marriages. They opposed child marriages, the Devadasi (temple courtesan) system and untouchability. They wanted to end the domination of Brahmins over other sections of the society in all spheres of life. As a symbol of their opposition to Varnashrama dharma, the Self-Respecters burned the *Manusmriti*[9] publicly in many places. The movement had an atheistic tint[10] even in the early days and was outspoken in its criticism of Hindu religious rituals. It published pamphlets like 'Visithira Devarkal Kortu' (the Trial of Weird Gods) in which various Hindu deities were denounced in the form of a mock trial.

In late 1927, Rajaji made a final attempt to bring Periyar back into the fold of the Congress. He arranged for Periyar to meet with Gandhi, who was on a visit to Bangalore (now Bengaluru). Though he was out of the Congress, Periyar still held Gandhi in high regard. He placed three demands before Gandhi—the Congress, the Hindu religion and the domination of Brahmins had to be destroyed. Gandhi did not accept any of them. A frustrated Periyar renounced his earlier respect for

Gandhi and started thinking of him as an ideological foe. It was at this point he stopped referring to Gandhi as 'Mahatma'.

The Movement Grows

The Subbarayan ministry was being pulled apart due to internal differences. When the Simon Commission visited India in 1928 to examine the working of the diarchal system, the nationalists boycotted it. Subbarayan was against the boycott, but his cabinet was for it. The Justice Party, too, initially intended boycotting the commission. But with Swarajists supporting the boycott, the Justicites soon changed their mind and announced that they welcomed the commission. Periyar too was favourably inclined toward the commission.

Subbarayan's government survived with the support of the Justice Party. He replaced his ministers with members who crossed over from the Swaraj Party. S. Muthiah Mudaliar, one of the new ministers, was a supporter of communal representation. The new cabinet soon issued a government order for implementing the communal representation legislation passed six years earlier in 1921. It did not go as far as Periyar had wished for,[11] but it did reserve forty-four per cent of the seats for non-Brahmins in educational institutions and government jobs.[12] Periyar accepted the compromise and praised Mudaliar in *Kudi Arasu* for making his dream of reservation a reality.

Meanwhile, the Self-Respect Movement was growing by leaps and bounds. On 7 November 1928, Periyar began a new English periodical named *Revolt*[13] to carry its message to all sections of the society. On 17 February 1929, the first provincial conference of the movement was held in Chengelpet. In the conference, resolutions supporting widow remarriage, inter-caste marriage and condemning donation of money for rituals in temples were passed. More than three thousand people, including the Chief Minister Subbarayan, attended it. Speaking at the conference, Periyar announced the removal of the caste suffix 'Naicker' from his name as a symbol of renouncing caste. It was an extremely bold act during a time when almost everyone used a caste suffix; Periyar was putting his principles to practice.

Reforming Weddings

Periyar understood that inter-caste marriages were essential for creating a casteless society. The traditional wedding and its associated rituals were a barrier for people wishing to marry outside their castes. Their traditions also prohibited widow remarriage. To facilitate such marriages, Periyar devised a new rationalist marriage system called the 'Self-Respect marriage'.

From 1928, he began organizing these new weddings all over the Tamil speaking districts of the state. They were conducted without any Brahmin priests or chanting of the ritual Sanskrit hymns. They were often deliberately conducted in times considered inauspicious (Rahu Kaalam). Some even took place at midnight. They did away with the thali-tying ceremony and instead had the couple taking oaths promising to treat each other equally and as friends.

The new style of marriage was a novelty and soon, many people belonging to different castes adopted it. There were even a few Muslim couples who got married in the new way. This method was also used to conduct widow remarriages. Often, such weddings were used as mass events to popularize the new movement. Activists—especially women—addressed the audience about the ideals and goals of the movement. *Kudi Arasu* reported these extensively. The audience was encouraged to ask questions on subjects like the man-woman relationship, marriage and women's emancipation.

Periyar did not consider all marriages that did away with rituals as Self-Respect marriages. Only those in which the equality of sexes was pledged were considered Self-Respect marriages. Between 1928 and 1932, more than eight thousand such weddings were organized.

Women and the Self-Respect Movement

The Self-Respect Movement's stance on women was far ahead of its times and outraged many conservatives. The Self-Respecters demanded equality of the sexes in all spheres of life. They wanted equal property rights, advocated sexual freedom and endorsed contraception. Periyar went as far as denouncing the concept of chastity which he believed was a tool of male oppression.

The Congress, too, had been advocating women's rights for some time. But there was a huge difference between the approaches of the two parties. In the Congress, men spoke for women and decided which rights should be demanded for them. They advised husbands, instead of wives, on how to handle issues like contraception and family planning. But in the Self-Respect Movement, it was the women who did all the talking and they targeted wives instead of husbands.

According to Periyar, men struggling for women's rights would only serve to handicap them even more—women had to be encouraged to take their destiny in their own hands. In the Self-Respect Movement, women conducted their own meetings and made all the major decisions on the women's rights front. There were even separate conferences to address women's problems.

The seminal pamphlet—'Penn yaen adimaiyanaal?' (Why did women become enslaved?)—published by Periyar in 1928 was a clarion call for women's rights. It laid down the reforms he was seeking to achieve—abolition of child marriages, compulsory registration of marriages, a divorce act and even acceptance of polyandry. He denounced the notions of chastity and pativrata (obedience to husbands). Later, Periyar would even advocate the concept of test tube babies for liberating women from the burden and restrictions of reproduction.

By 1929, the Self-Respect Movement had a footprint in almost all Tamil speaking districts of the state. Its growth had been rapid due to a well-organized propaganda machinery and generous financial backing from non-Brahmin industrialists and landowners. With its stable of Tamil periodicals, led by the flagship *Kudi Arasu*, the movement was able to reach a wider audience. Pamphlets, songs, slogans and skits were used to spread the word.

In 1930, the Self-Respecters began a campaign against the Devadasi practice. Moovalur Ramamirtham, a Self-Respecter, who had been a Devadasi herself, was at the forefront of the campaign. A bill for abolishing the practice was tabled in the legislative council by the state's first female legislator, Dr Muthulakshmi Reddy. It ran into heavy opposition from the traditionalists like Congress leader S. Satyamurti. Many in the Justice Party too opposed the bill.

Ramamirtham and Periyar backed Muthulakshmi against the traditionalists. When Satyamurti argued for keeping the tradition alive, Muthulakshmi created a sensation by asking him to send his daughter to be trained as a courtesan instead. However, the bill was defeated in the council due to lack of support.[14]

Around this time, Periyar got into a huge controversy for

encouraging Adi-Dravidas (Dalits) to convert to Islam. He had to issue a lengthy explanation in *Kudi Arasu* for his stance on conversion. He reasoned that Islam was the only religion that did not discriminate on the basis of birth and for an Adi-Dravida, conversion would offer a way to shed his shackles and live a dignified life.

Periyar's fame as a radical reformer was spreading. He received invitations from Tamils in Burma, Malaysia and Singapore to visit and address meetings. In December 1929, he departed on a month-long trip to the Southeast Asian countries. He addressed several well-attended public meetings in Malaysia and Singapore. There was a brief campaign by the periodical, *Tamil Nesan*, to ban him from visiting Malaysia claiming that he was a rabble-rousing radical. But the attempt failed and the trip was a success. It made Periyar well known among the Tamil diaspora as a social reformer. He returned to India in time for the 1930 election campaign.

The Congress and Swarajists boycotted the election and the Periyar-backed Justice Party won easily. But it proved to be the swan song of the non-Brahmin party. Times were changing and a nationalistic fervour was sweeping the nation. Against it, the voice of social reform lost its appeal and the Congress was on the rise.

4
Flirting with Socialism

How can there be any progress without political or economic reforms? A Self-Respect Movement which ignores them and concentrates only on exposing the foolishness of old epics and Brahminical plots is useless.

—From Periyar's speech
Thirupatthur Conference, 1933 (VIII: c3)

1931 was a year of great change for Periyar and the Self-Respect Movement. They were slowly drifting apart from the Justice Party. The Self-Respecters were upset that the Justice Party had treated them as mere instruments for obtaining power and neglected their demands after attaining it. They were also regularly getting into trouble with the police. The Congress' Civil-Disobedience movement was at its peak then. The execution of Bhagat Singh and his comrades in the Lahore conspiracy case had kindled revolutionary fervour amongst the youth. Nationalist feelings were running high among the populace and the Justice Party's reputation as

British collaborators was making it unpopular. The Congress was occupying the nationalist space in the political spectrum. Periyar's dislike of all things Gandhian and related to the Congress party wouldn't let him touch them with a bargepole. Thus, when the rank and file of the party shifted toward nationalism, he tried to steer it away from the Congress.

A New Direction

Periyar was looking for a new direction for the party and he found it in socialism. The Self-Respect Movement adopted rationalism because of its anti-Varnashrama and anti-Brahmin political ideology. But its turn towards socialism was purely due to political pragmatism. To attract the nationalistic-minded youth, they started getting closer to the communists. While moving toward new ideals, Periyar ensured that their anti-Congress nature remained undiluted.

The move towards rationalism and socialism did come at a cost. The rich industrialists who had been bankrolling the Self-Respect Movement were not amused by it. They did not like the overt atheism of the movement and the virulent attacks on religion in their journals and public speeches. W.P.A. Soundara Pandiyan Nadar,[15] V.V. Ramasamy Nadar and R.K. Shanmugam Chettiar[16] were the main supporters of Periyar at that time. The outspoken atheism of Periyar made Chettiar walk out of the movement's third provincial conference held at Virudhunagar in August 1931. Before the end of the year, the Nadars too had cut off their financial support to the movement.

Periyar's newfound friendship with the communists made him look towards the Soviet Union for inspiration. He wanted to see for himself how the socialist ideal worked when put to practice. On 13 December 1931, he departed on a tour of

Europe and Russia. On the voyage, he spent a few days each in South Africa, Turkey and Greece. He reached the Soviet Union on 13 February 1932.

The world was in the grip of the Great Depression[17] then. Militant labour movements were the flavour of the day. In the Soviet Union, he was hosted by the Soviet government, various youth communes, unions and atheist organizations. He visited many cities, colleges and factories. He lived among the workers and learnt how the socialist soviet society functioned. Highly impressed, he applied for the membership of the Communist Party. But for some reason, the Soviet authorities became suspicious of his companion S. Ramanathan and expelled both of them from the country on 19 May 1932. However, this disappointing exit did not diminish Periyar's admiration for socialism.

He spent the next few months visiting England, Germany, Spain, Portugal and France. While in England, he fell in with trade unionists like Shapurji Saklatwala.[18] He attended their meetings and visited their factories. He even addressed a labour meeting on 20 June 1932 at Malmesbury Park in Yorkshire. In his speech, he denounced Ramsay Macdonald's Labour Party government for being insensitive to the needs of the Indian labour class. He returned to India in November 1932, after a brief stay in Sri Lanka, where he made a whirlwind tour delivering speeches in eighteen towns in the span of three weeks.

While he was in Europe, his movement continued its leftward drift. Abandoned by its rich supporters, it attracted communists like M. Singaravelu Chettiar, who soon won the admiration of the Self-Respecters. When Periyar returned to India, he found the movement's attitude toward socialism to be similar to his own. But a few of his old associates like S. Ramanathan and Sami Chidambaram[19] did not want to dilute the movement's social reform plank. At a meeting convened at his house on 28 December 1932, Periyar struck a balance between the two groups. The movement would continue to preach social reform. At the same time, socialism would also be adopted on an official platform. He formed the Self-Respect Socialist Party (Suya Mariyadhai Samadharma Katchi) as a separate entity to promote socialism. He planned to use it as a vehicle for contesting elections and achieving his political goals. He formulated the famed 'Erode Programme' outlining the newly re-organized movement's goals. The programme declared the following as the goals of the party: (XV: p77)

- Debts of the farmers should be immediately written off and steps taken to prevent them from falling into debt again.
- Usury should be banned and banks that provide loans against lands should be opened in large numbers.
- Land ownership through benamis (proxies) should be banned.
- The government should eliminate middlemen and make arrangements for the farmers to sell their produce directly to consumers.
- Plans should be drawn up to provide primary education to all within a specified period.
- Prohibition should be enforced.
- Appropriate measures should be taken to abolish untouchability and other superstitions.

Socialism Embraced and Abandoned

The year 1933 saw the Self-Respect Movement embracing socialism wholeheartedly. It organized May Day celebrations and published books and pamphlets on socialism through *Kudi Arasu*. Marxist tracts by Frederich Engels and other Russian authors were translated into Tamil and published by the movement's Unmai Vilakkam publications. A socialist conference was convened under Singaravelu Chettiar's leadership at Mannargudi. Periyar, who had shunned electoral politics during his days in the Congress, was now running a political party with socialist ideals.

Congress, too, had been bitten by the socialist bug and had started adopting similar policies. But Periyar made sure that his new party maintained an anti-Congress and anti-Justice Party stand. While he was busy promoting socialism and his new party, Periyar suffered a personal tragedy.

His wife Nagammal fell ill and died on 11 May 1933. He arranged for her body to be put in a coffin, carried in a hearse and then cremated. Using a coffin was an Islamic tradition, the hearse a Christian ritual and cremation a Hindu rite. True to his principles, he managed to combine the funeral customs of Muslims, Christians and Hindus for his wife. He paid a glowing tribute to her three days later in an obituary in *Kudi Arasu*.

Then, in December 1933, the government struck him hard. It arrested Periyar for publishing an editorial titled, 'Why this government must be destroyed' in *Kudi Arasu*.[20] The magazine's publisher, Periyar's sister Kannamma, was fined two thousand rupees. *Kudi Arasu* had to cease publication temporarily. An unfazed Periyar started publishing another magazine, *Puratchi* (Revolt), in its place. Ironically, the government that jailed him was a Justice Party government led by the Raja of Bobbili,[21] whom the Self-Respecters had helped become chief minister.[22]

Periyar was found guilty under section 124 of the IPC[23] and sentenced to six months' imprisonment in the Coimbatore jail; he found himself in the cell next to that of his old rival, Rajaji. Rajaji was there because of his participation in the Salt Satyagraha. The two men tried to bridge their differences. Periyar pitched the Erode Programme to Rajaji, but insisted that the Congress accept communal representation as official policy. But the effort went nowhere as Gandhi rejected the idea firmly. When Periyar was released, his supporters were jubilant. But he himself was nonplussed:

> I did not go to jail for doing anything significant. I went to jail for writing an ordinary editorial. If the government had bothered to read the back issues of *Kudi Arasu*, it would have found enough seditious material to exile me. (XV: p76)

His wish came true soon. Alarmed with the increasing revolutionary activity in the country, the colonial administration banned the Communist Party of India in July 1934. The Young Worker's League, a communist affiliated organization, too, was banned later. The Self-Respect Movement faced a similar fate because of its avowed socialism. Surveillance and harassment by intelligence agents became commonplace for Self-Respecters. Periyar was arrested again in 1934 for publishing a Tamil translation of Bhagat Singh's pamphlet, 'Why I am an atheist'. He had to tender an apology to the government to secure his release. *Puratchi* was banned for carrying an article by P. Jeevanandam[24] titled 'Blind Capitalists and the Deaf Government'. Periyar first responded by starting a new journal, *Pagutharivu* (Rationalism), but that too came under government scrutiny.

The government crackdown had its effect. To ensure political survival, Periyar decided to move the Self-Respect Movement away from communism. He reasoned:

I will not go to jail as a hero and destroy the Self-Respect movement. There is no other alternative to our movement in this country for destroying caste. (X: p28)

Both the Congress and the Justice Party sent out feelers to him. Congress leader Jayaprakash Narayan tried to convince him to merge the Self-Respect Movement with the Congress Socialist Party.[25] Arcot Ramasamy Mudaliar of the Justice Party also offered him a chance to campaign for them in the 1934 council elections. The Justic Party was in a bad shape politically. The landlord faction led by the Raja of Bobbili had alienated the party from the people by its autocratic approach to governance leading to the party's desperate need for a mass campaigner.

Periyar sent his Erode Programme to both the parties with the condition that whoever accepted and assured its implementation would get his support. While the Congress hesitated due to the programme's anti-caste clauses, a desperate Bobbili accepted immediately and formed a committee for implementing it. Periyar decided to throw in his lot with the Justice Party. In October 1934, he officially announced his support for the party. But his support was too late to save the Justice government—they lost the 1934 elections. But as the Congress refused to take power under the diarchal system, Bobbili managed to hang on as chief minister by forming a minority government. It was around this time that Periyar first met a young college student named C.N. Annadurai (Anna),[26] who would go on to become his protégé and later, a bitter rival.

The decision to go back to the Justice camp and the subsequent loss at the election shook the Self-Respect Movement badly. His former communist disciples were angry with him. At the party conference at Thiruthuraipoondi in February 1935, Jeevanandam led a revolt against Periyar, forcing him to leave the conference midway. In April 1935, the Communist sympathizers split from the movement and formed their own 'Self Respect Socialist Party', which eventually merged with the Congress Socialist Party. Periyar consoled the Justice Party members and calmed them down:

> Contesting elections is a gamble. We should learn to take the losses in our stride. My dear non-Brahmin youth, let this loss be a lesson for you. Thank the Brahmins for this loss, for they have taught us a valuable lesson. (XV: p 78)

The fling with the Communists was over. Periyar was back with the Justicites and spent the next few years trying to repair the damage done to the movement by the loss of the communists.

5
The Language War

Public Prosecutor: You have small children. If you go to prison, you will suffer there and your husband too will suffer [at home]. Promise not to participate in the agitations hereafter and we will let you go free.

Woman Prisoner: For the progress of our language and our nation, we [the women] are willing to suffer anything. Our husbands have no right to stop us.

—Exchange in a Madras Court
Kudi Arasu, 20 November 1938

For encouraging women to court arrest and speak as shown above, Periyar was sentenced to a year of rigorous imprisonment and fined one thousand rupees in 1938. The Madras Presidency was aflame with anti-Hindi feelings and the Self-Respect Movement had obtained a new lease of life. Ironically, the credit for reviving the once sagging fortunes of the movement belonged to Periyar's old rival, Rajaji, who was now the chief minister of the presidency.

The Decline of Justice Party

Four years earlier, reeling from the British government's harassment, Periyar had been forced to take up the unwanted role of being the propagandist for a highly unpopular Justice Party. Not only did Justice lose the 1934 council elections, but it also got trounced in the assembly elections three years later. Driven by factionalism and beset with nepotism, the Justice Party was falling apart gradually. The landlord faction controlling the party was alienating popular support by adopting harsh economic measures during the Great Depression. One by one, the classes which formed the party's traditional support base became disillusioned and abandoned it. Even the European establishment, which valued the party for its loyalty to the British crown, became disgusted by the inept and corrupt administration of the Raja of Bobbili.

The Justicites refused to support the Debt Relief Act, which would have reduced the burden of land tax on the peasants. When the Congress organized protests demanding tax relief for peasants, Bobbili cracked down hard on them. Similarly, when weavers who had lost their livelihoods due to the economic recession demanded debt relief, the government used repressive measures against them. While the Congress was endearing itself to the working class of the state, the Justice leaders were doing just the opposite—disillusioning their former supporters by living opulently.[27] Hatred for the Justicites was palpable amongst the populace. As the governor of Madras, Lord Erskine, put it to the secretary of state for India, Marquess Zetland, 'every sin of omission or commission of the past fifteen years is put down to them [Justicites].'

The Government of India Act, 1935, ushered in provincial autonomy in British India and gave more powers to the

Indian legislatures than the previous diarchal system.[28] During 1935–36, the rise of the Congress became evident thanks to a string of victories in local body elections. With the detested diarchal system gone, the Congress was free to abandon its policy of non-participation in the government.

Elections under the new provincial autonomy system were scheduled for February 1937. The Congress put out a populist manifesto promising something to each and every section of the society. The rising popularity of the Congress was not lost on the Justicites. Many of them abandoned the party and crossed over to the Congress to ensure political survival. A few like the Raja of Pithapuram and M.A. Muthiah Chettiar left to form their own political party (The People's Party of Madras). Only Periyar and the Self-Respect Movement stuck doggedly to the sinking Justice ship. And the compensation for their continued support was the adoption of the Erode Programme, which ironically had a lot of ideals unacceptable to the Justice Party's landlords.

Periyar was also given editorial control of the Justice-sponsored journal *Viduthalai* (Freedom). But Periyar's support was not enough to stop the drubbing the Justice Party received in the election. The Congress achieved an outstanding victory, taking 159 of the 215 assembly seats and 27 of the 46 council seats. Incumbent Justice leaders including Bobbili, A.P. Patro, the Raja of Ramnad, and P.T. Rajan lost. Throughout India, Congress had won in eight provinces, but it refused to form governments. It did not like the veto powers given to the colonial governor by the Government of India Act, 1935. For three months, they refused to take power while the veto remained in place. In Madras, the governor formed an interim government under the Justice leader K.V. Reddi Naidu. Three months later, the Congress caved in, accepted Viceroy

Linlithgow's assurance that the discretionary powers would not be misused and formed the government. Congress formed the new government in July 1937 and Rajaji became the new prime minister (the first minister's post was called 'prime minister' or 'premier' in the period between 1937–47). Periyar ridiculed the new ministry as the 'ministry that surrendered'.

The Anti-Hindi Agitation

When the morale of the Self-Respect Movement was at an all-time low and the Justice Party was in disarray, Rajaji unwittingly helped revitalize the movement—he introduced compulsory learning of Hindi in the presidency's schools. The Congress' obsession with Hindi had its roots in Gandhi's belief that Hindi would be able to unite Indians linguistically against the colonial power.[29] However, they did not take into account the fierce linguistic pride of the Tamils and the reaction this move would have on them. In April 1938, Hindi was made a subject for Forms 1 to 3[30] in 125 secondary schools in the presidency. Periyar took the lead in opposing Hindi in the state and the Justice Party rallied behind him. Bobbili was then on a long private tour of Europe and A.T. Pannirselvam[31] was one of the few remaining effective Justice leaders. Periyar and Pannirselvam coordinated their actions against the Hindi policy.

Rajaji had failed to judge the depth of the feeling against Hindi in the state. The first to flock to the banner of protest were the Shaivites,[32] who regarded Tamil as divine and the mandatory teaching of Hindi as an attempt to destroy it. Ironically, the Shaivites had been implacable foes of the Self-Respect Movement because of its atheism and its tendency to ridicule the epics they held sacred. Now they were helping Periyar in his struggle against Hindi. Professors like Somasundara Bharathi,

Maraimalai Adigal,[33] Mudiyarasan and Illakuvanar also threw in their support.

The Justice members of the legislature (conveniently ignoring the fact that it had been their government which had first introduced Hindi in the schools earlier in 1931), argued in the Assembly against the mandatory Hindi rule. Tamil-speaking Muslims of the state also joined the anti-Hindi agitation. Though Urdu-speaking Muslims supported Hindi, a few of them like Muslim Leaguer P. Khalifullah joined the anti-Hindi bandwagon. Between August 1937 (when Rajaji first proposed to introduce mandatory Hindi in a policy note) and April 1938 (when he issued the formal government order), a formidable anti-Hindi coalition had formed under Periyar's leadership. The election defeat of 1937 was forgotten and the movement had found a new mission.

The Self-Respecters were no strangers to politics of agitation. They soon launched a programme of picketing government schools and offices, organizing fasts, processions, black flag marches and conferences to protest the Hindi order. Periyar deftly tapped into the anti-Brahmin suspicions of the general population. He warned that ninety per cent of the non-Brahmin children would fail their exams if Hindi was made mandatory. He accused Rajaji of attempting to make Tamils subservient to the Hindi imperialists of North India. *Kudi Arasu* carried cartoons titled 'Acharyar Sagasam' (The misadventures of the acharya) depicting Rajaji as a villain trying to stab Tamil Thai (mother Tamil) and even disrobing her. Indefinite fasts outside Rajaji's official residence became commonplace. Other actions of Rajaji played into the hands of Periyar. Rajaji had to close down 2,200 primary schools in the state due to the financial crunch caused by the imposition of prohibition. But at the same time, he sanctioned the opening of a vedpadshala

(Vedic instruction school) at the cost of twelve lakh rupees. This was seized upon by the agitators as further proof that Rajaji was playing with the futures of non-Brahmin children. Periyar's strategy paid off and the agitation gained momentum across the state. In August 1938, he flagged off a march by the Thamilar Padai (Tamil Army) from Trichy. Led by Anja Nenjan (Brave Heart) Pattukottai Azhagiri[34] and Moovalur Ramamirtham, the agitators visited towns and villages along the way, spreading their anti-Hindi message. When they reached Madras in September, a rousing reception awaited them at the Triplicane beach. They had succeeded in raising popular support for the anti-Hindi agitation. By now, the Justice Party machinery was effectively in the hands of Periyar.

Till October 1938, the agitation had been peaceful and deemed ineffectual by the government. But in that month, its intensity increased following Periyar's direct involvement in organizing the protests. His fiery speeches denouncing Brahmins and Hindi whipped up the population. He also mobilized women in support of the agitation. Women started participating in numbers never seen before in a political agitation. He convened a women's conference at Vellore in November to demonstrate women's opposition to Hindi. On 14 November, the first of the seventy-two women who would eventually go to jail for participating in the agitation were arrested. Many of the arrested women had young children and chose to go to jail with them.

The provincial government was exasperated by the women's participation. It was a completely new situation for them. On 21 November, an anti-Hindi procession in George Town, Madras turned violent and the agitators started pelting stones at shops and offices. Rajaji cracked down immediately on the movement. Periyar was arrested and put on trial for 'inciting women to disobey the law'. He was sentenced to one year in jail and asked to pay a fine of a thousand rupees. To pay the fine, he had to sell his Ford motor car.

It was during his time in jail that the Progressive Women's Association gave him the title Periyar (The Great Elder). By the end of 1938, Periyar's takeover of the Justice Party was nearly complete. Pannirselvam had withdrawn from provincial politics and was preparing to go to London to take up a seat in the India Council. Periyar smoothly filled the vacuum created by the loss of effective leadership and was elected formally as the president of the party. This happened during a three-day conference of the Justice Party held between 29–31 December 1938 while he was still in prison. An empty chair was kept on the conference dais to symbolize his presence.

With Periyar in jail, the agitation took a more militant turn under the leadership of the second-rung leaders like Annadurai. The protesters soon started provoking a disproportionate response from the police. The number of agitators being arrested for picketing increased. Two of them—Thalamuthu and Natarajan—died in prison in early 1939 and became the first martyrs of the language agitation. Both had been arrested picketing government institutions and both died of ailments while in jail. Their funeral processions became recruiting grounds for the agitation and their deaths were debated fiercely in the Assembly. But Rajaji did not heed the protesters; he was still dismissive of them. He started using the Criminal Law Amendment Act of 1932 against the agitators, so that they could be arrested for 'non-bailable' offences.

Rajaji's increasingly authoritarian attitude had the Congress worried. The Criminal Law Act had been originally enacted by the colonial government to crush the Congress' Non-Cooperation Movement in the early 1930s. Many in the

Congress, like Satyamurti, were uneasy with the party itself using such a draconian law against civilians. He advised Rajaji to make Hindi an optional subject and thus deprive the agitators of a cause to create trouble. He was supported by Sarvepalli Radhakrishnan[35] and T.T. Krishnamachari. But Rajaji did not listen to them. Even Governor Erskine, a typical colonial administrator, was taken aback by Rajaji's authoritarianism.

In May 1939, Periyar was released early from jail on medical grounds. The agitation and the arrests continued unabated till September 1939. By then, around 1,200 protestors had been arrested and thrown in jail.

Rajaji's Congress government resigned on 29 October 1939. They were protesting the colonial administration involving India in the newly-declared Second World War without consulting them first.[36] Madras Presidency was placed under the direct rule of the governor. Governor Erskine was more sympathetic to the anti-Hindi movement than Rajaji had been. When Hindi was first introduced, he had written to Viceroy Linlithgow, saying, 'compulsory Hindi has been the cause of great trouble in this province and is certainly contrary to the wishes of the bulk of the population.'

The day after Rajaji's resignation, Periyar suspended the agitation and asked the governor to rescind the mandatory Hindi rule. On 21 February 1940, the governor made Hindi an optional subject in schools. Thus, the first language war ended with a victory for Periyar and the Self-Respect Movement.

6
Promised Lands

Indians want self-determination and the right to decide their future. Similarly we, the Dravidians, want to decide the future of Dravida Nadu. If we had had this right to self determination in the past, we wouldn't be in this disgraceful state of calling ourselves bastards and Sudras. If this pathetic self-loathing is to end, we need the power to decide our fates.

—Periyar in *Kudi Arasu*, 11 February 1940

The anti-Hindi agitation spawned a new slogan for the resurgent Justice Party—'Tamil Nadu for the Tamils'. Periyar coined it during the reception for the 'Tamil Army' at Madras in September 1938. The idea of a separate South Indian state goes even further back. As early as 1930, Periyar had questioned the notion of India being a single monolithic country in a public meeting of the Self-Respect Movement. In December 1937, when the opponents of Hindi first got together at a public anti-Hindi meeting in Velur, a resolution had been passed demanding a separate province for

Tamil-speaking people. The agitation against Hindi (viewed by the Justicites as a North Indian import) progressed to the next logical stage—demanding secession.

A Confusing Idea

The imposition of Hindi by the Congress government confirmed the secessionists' fears. Periyar believed that the Congress party was a tool in the hands of the North Indians and Brahmins. He felt that the Tamils would be treated fairly only if they had a nation of their own. The initial secessionist demand was for a separate state for the Tamils. But it soon morphed into a demand for Dravida Nadu—a federation of areas where the four major Dravidian languages[37] were spoken. Periyar declared all the people who lived in those areas—except Brahmins—as Dravidians. There was some confusion over whether he had dropped the 'Tamil Nadu' demand altogether. But soon he explained that he viewed Malayalees, Kannadigas and Telugus as Tamils and in his view 'Dravidam and Tamil Nadu were one and the same'.

The party designed a new Tamil flag featuring the emblems of the three ancient Tamil kingdoms[38] and used it in its processions in the anti-Hindi agitation. Periyar's anti-Brahmin rhetoric was hard to swallow for the Justice Party 'old guard'. Facing criticism from European newspapers like the *Madras Mail*, A.T. Pannirselvem was forced to clarify that Brahmins would not be driven away from the new state as it had enough space for both Aryans from North India and English speakers from the West. But they would be allowed to stay only as settlers.

Periyar hoped that the idea of Dravida Nadu would engage the public's imagination like Jinnah's demand for a separate state for Muslims. But support for Dravida Nadu among Tamils was nowhere near the Muslim support for Pakistan.

In January 1940, he visited Bombay (now Mumbai) and met Jinnah and B.R. Ambedkar to canvass support for his secessionist campaign. He wanted to form a general anti-Congress alliance with them. Anna served as his interpreter. Addressing a public meeting at Dharavi on 7 January, he said that Tamil Nadu was as big as Germany and had a population equal to that of England. He asked for Ambedkar's and Jinnah's support for the new nation. Though Periyar returned home claiming he had won Jinnah's support for Dravida Nadu, Jinnah's response was lukewarm. Though he initially made some public utterances supporting Dravida Nadu, he declined outright to extend his support to Periyar later in 1944.

The first half of 1940 was spent in a flurry of conferences and meetings promoting Dravida Nadu. With the Congress back in opposition, the British government was favourably inclined towards the Justice Party. They even offered Periyar the chance to form a government. But he declined to accept power. Examples of the goodwill that existed between both sides can be found in his speeches during that period. Periyar even publicly appealed to the British to stay in India till the Dravidians were ready to defend themselves from Aryan aggression. The party even observed a 'Separation of India Day' on 19 April.

On 2 June, Periyar unveiled the map of the proposed state at the Dravida Nadu conference at Kanchipuram. It showed the whole of South India and even parts of Bengal. Speakers at the conference accused the Congress of colluding with Hitler's Nazi regime and planning to subjugate Dravidians under Aryan rule.

The secessionist idea was neither clear nor well thought out. Rather than making a clear case for gaining power, Periyar was pitching the new state as a means for social reform. The idea did not gain sufficient traction with the people. It completely failed to garner support in the non-Tamil areas of the Madras province. Periyar was forced to clarify that if non-Tamil Dravidians did not want a separate nation, then the two crore Tamil population would go for a separate state alone.

In August 1941, Periyar announced the suspension of the Dravida Nadu agitation as a show of support to the British government in the Second World War. When the Cripps mission[39] visited India in 1942, to pitch constitutional reform to the Indians, a Justice delegation comprising W.P.A. Soundarapandian Nadar, N.R. Samiappa Mudaliar, M.A. Muthiah Chettiar and Periyar met them in Madras seeking its support for Dravida Nadu. But Strafford Cripps bluntly refused to consider the idea and advised them to seek a general referendum or a resolution in the Madras legislature. With this rejection, any chance of gaining official British sanction for Dravida Nadu was gone. The new state would have to be wrested from the Congress when it eventually became the master of independent India.

When the Cripps mission failed, the Congress launched the Quit India Movement demanding full independence. Periyar did not join them and even announced he would start an 'Ariyanae Veliyeru' (Aryans Get Out) campaign on similar lines.

A Literary Interlude

Though Periyar kept the Dravida Nadu issue alive during the next few years, he turned his focus to literary issues. He felt that the old shastras and puranas were the reasons for the docile behaviour of the Tamil people.

In 1942, in an attempt to discredit the old literary

works, he chose two among them and announced that they would be burned for belittling Tamils. The Ramayana and Periyapuranam,[40] the two unfortunate works to be chosen, were beholden to Vaishnavites and Shaivites respectively. The goodwill between the Shaivites and the Self-Respect Movement evaporated as soon as Periyar chose Periyapuranam as a target. Periyar did not like the portrayal of Saint Nandan[41] as a farm labourer who becomes a Brahmin after undergoing 'purification' by self-immolation. He saw it as a typical trick by the Brahmins. He viewed the burning of Nandan as a symbol of the subjugation of the Sudras by the Brahmins.

Ramayana came in for a more savage criticism from the Self-Respecters. Periyar had earlier written an alternate version of the Ramayana,[42] where he had offered a fresh new perspective on the story of Rama. Contrary to the usual practice, he had depicted Rama as a villain, while extolling the virtues of the Rakshasa king Ravana.[43] Influenced by his thoughts, Pulavar Kuzhandhai, a poet with Dravidian leanings, wrote the *Ravana Kaaviyam* (The Epic of Ravana), which portrayed Ravana as the hero and Rama as the villain.

At Periyar's insistence, Anna published a series of literary critiques titled *Kamba Rasam* (The Essence of Kamban), on the poet Kamban's version of the Ramayana in 1943. It was a venomous critique accusing Kamban of vulgar taste and promoting obscenities. Even Anna thought it was too severe. He told his friends to look at it only as a propaganda piece rather than genuine literary criticism. Anna also wrote a satirical commentary called *Needhi Devan Mayakkam* (Justice's Dilemma) in which Ravana conducts an imaginary trial of Kamban for slandering his character.

The campaign against the epics was part of a broader war against all things North Indian and Aryan. Periyar sought to turn the Tamil people against what he viewed as symbols of Aryan (and Brahmin) oppression. While he did not succeed in demonizing Rama, he did partially succeed in resurrecting Ravana as a champion of Dravidians.

The Power Struggle

While Periyar was campaigning for a separate state and against ancient epics, the 'old guard' of the Justice Party was having second thoughts about where he was leading them. For a party long accustomed to the cushy life of power and patronage, the strain and pace of frequent protests and agitations were too much to handle. They did not like this new non-political version of the party at all. They were also uneasy with many aspects of the social reforms Periyar was advocating. They were happy with taking jobs away from the Brahmins and redistributing them among the non-Brahmins, but they were put off by some of the more militant ideals of Periyar. For his part, Periyar viewed them as people whose time had come and gone. He did not share their hankering for power and adulation for the British. More than anything, he wanted to do away with the 'British-friendly' image of the party. The Congress had successfully portrayed the Justice Party as anti-national (with good cause) and the label had stuck. Periyar wanted to get rid of that taint.

Throughout 1943 and the first half of 1944, both Periyar and the 'old guard' tried to manoeuvre each other out of power. The clash of factions culminated in an explosive climax at Salem in August 1944. When the party suffered a series of electoral defeats in the mid-1930s, a large number of its leaders left the party to join the Congress. Interested in maintaining their positions of power, they had thought they were hitching their wagons to the rising star of the Congress. But, after two years in power, the Congress resigned and went back to opposing the colonial government. Those who had joined the Congress in the hope of maintaining their positions were now stuck. When Periyar took over the Justice Party, they hoped that he would soon participate in the government, and came back to rejoin it.

Contrary to their expectations, Periyar remained steadfast in his opposition to taking part in the government. Twice he was offered the chance to become prime minister of the province and both the times he declined it. The businessmen and landlords, who were the main financial backers of the party, were also not comfortable with the newfound activism. They did not want to jeopardize their commercial interests by advocating unpopular social reforms.

The first serious revolt against Periyar's leadership had come as early as 1940, when K.A.P. Viswanatham, the party's general secretary, quit due to differences with him. Anna replaced him as general secretary and the issue died down quickly. The party's 'old guard' made a serious attempt to oust Periyar from the party leadership in 1944. His term as party president was coming to an end and the new leader was to be elected at the party's sixteenth annual conference. The 'old guard' comprised P. Balasubramaniam, C.G. Netto, A.P. Patro, C.L. Narasimha Mudaliar, Damodaran Naidu, R.K. Shanmugam Chettiar, P.T. Rajan and K.V. Rethinasamy.[44] A few others like W.P.A. Soundarapandian Nadar were caught between the dissidents and Periyar's radicals. The 'old guards' planned to oppose Periyar's re-election as party president and started looking for a suitable candidate to run against him.[45] They even made overtures to Anna to join their side.

The sixteenth conference held at Salem on 27 August 1944 became the scene of the power struggle. To counter the dissidents, Periyar unveiled an ambitious plan for revamping the party. With his backing, Anna proposed some path-breaking resolutions (XV: p90, X: p93, XXII: p22-23):

- Party members—both current and those wanting to join in the future—must renounce the government's honourary titles like Rao Bahadur and Diwan Bahadur.
- They must immediately resign from their honourary and appointed government posts.
- They must not contest any elections conducted by the government.
- They must drop the caste suffixes from their names.

In short, the passage of the resolutions would mean a total acceptance of the Self-Respect ideology by the Justice Party. The debate on the resolutions raged on continuously for thirty-five hours. One by one, the members of the 'old guard' were ground down by Periyar's followers. They either left the dais or were convinced to back Periyar and Anna. In the end, Periyar emerged victorious—the party re-elected him and made him president for life. Then a new resolution was taken up about renaming the party. The party's actual name was South Indian Liberal Federation. The party came to be called 'Justice Party' after its popular periodical *Justice*. Now Periyar proposed that the name be changed to 'Dravidar Kazhagam'. Earlier, in a speech given at Sevvaipettai on 14 January 1944, he had explained the need for a new name:

> We lack a common symbol to represent our shared ideals and our institution. We are all Dravidians, we want a Dravida Nadu. The label 'Tamil' is too narrow to represent our diverse nature. Look around us—Kannappar here is a Telugu, I am a Kannadiga, and Annadurai is a Tamil. We have a thousand castes

amongst us. As for myself, I am ready to call myself a Tamil. But not all Kannadigas and Telugus will accept to do so. But they won't object to call themselves Dravidians and ask for a Dravida Nadu.

It is for this reason we should change the name to 'Dravidar Kazhagam'. Today even a Minister cannot escape the caste label. If we need to abolish caste, we need revolution, we need unity, we need discipline and most importantly, we need our own nation. We need political power to fulfil our goals, without it we would be struggling till the end of our days. For achieving all this we need to have 'Dravidian' as our unifying identity and 'Dravida Nadu' as our ultimate goal.

Thus the Justice Party became Dravidar Kazhagam. But not all of the 'old guard' accepted the change. Some of them led by B. Ramachandra Reddi[46] and P.T. Rajan left the party and insisted that they were the real Justice Party.[47] With a broadened appeal, the Dravidar Kazhagam was able to attract more than thirty thousand new members within a year of its formation. The goals and regulations of the newly unveiled party were formulated in a year's time and formally adopted in September 1945 (XV: p92). Some of them were:

1. (a) Dravida Nadu should have complete autonomy on its social, economic, industrial and commercial spheres.
    (b) Dravida Nadu and its citizens should be protected from the exploitation and influence of others.
2. (a) The citizens of Dravida Nadu should be given the opportunity to live and prosper without the distinctions of caste, class and hierarchy.
3. (a) The differences and superstitions that plague the Dravidian people in the name of religion and tradition

must be eradicated. Dravidians should be transformed into a society filled with generosity and knowledge.

(b) Till the above goals are achieved, we should secure the cooperation of the populace by earning their trust and goodwill. To this end we must get representation in various fields.

In 1946, the Dravidar Kazhagam adopted a new flag—a black square with a red circle at the centre (black representing the oppression of the Dravidians and red their rebellion against it). Not everyone in the new party was happy—behind the facade of this unity, trouble was brewing between Periyar and Anna.

7
The Big Split

Why should the leader of a Rationalist movement worry about inheritance? And why does a democratic organisation need an appointed heir? Are we running a jungle raj here?
—Anna's rebuttal to Periyar's wedding announcement in
Dravida Nadu,[48] 3 July 1949

On the outside, everything appeared normal in the newly-formed party. However, it was a different story inside—a silent struggle was going on between the party president and his heir presumptive—the general secretary. Annadurai (Anna) had long been accepted by the party members as the unofficial number two and man Friday to Periyar. The two men had first met in May 1935 when Anna was still a student at Pachaiyappa College in Madras. Already familiar with the patronage politics of the Justice Party, he had been attracted by the candour and freshness of Periyar's message.

By 1937, Anna had become a part of Periyar's inner circle. His admirable performance in the anti-Hindi agitations had catapulted him to the second most senior position. He was viewed by party members as someone more approachable than Periyar, who had a reputation for obstinacy.

The relationship between the two men was not always smooth. There were many differences of opinion between the two, but they always managed to work around them. Periyar did not completely trust his lieutenant. Even during the 1944 Salem conference, where he had wrested control of the party from the old guard with Anna's help, he had not been sure of where his protégé's real allegiance lay. He was not accustomed to having an underling who was held in the same regard as himself. The festering suspicion through which Periyar viewed Anna led to increasingly strained relations and ended with a split of the Dravidar Kazhagam in 1949. The split was the culmination of five years of discord and differences. In the long drawn-out battle between the two, three incidents stand out among others.

When Convention became Compulsion

The first was the black shirt issue. In the first provincial conference of Dravidar Kazhagam held at Trichy in September 1945, the new party put out its official rules and regulations. In that conference, Periyar announced the creation of a volunteer force called 'Dravidian Liberation Army' under E.V.K. Sampath[49] and poet S. Karunanandham. He also said that they should wear black shirts in order to be differentiated from other party volunteers.

Anna did not like the idea of 'black shirts'. He was not against the formation of a new volunteer force—he just did not want them to wear black. But he was in no mood to force the issue with Periyar. They had had one minor fight earlier—

Periyar had wanted to pass a resolution calling for boycott of Brahmin restaurants in the state and Anna convinced him to drop it as such a boycott would be impractical. This time, Anna came around and accepted the idea of wearing a black shirt half-heartedly.

Periyar, who was not accustomed to someone questioning his decisions, was miffed. He had thought that 'black shirts' would symbolize the oppression of Dravidians. And he wanted everyone in the party—men, women and volunteers—to start wearing black to express opposition to their oppression. But Anna felt that it was enough if volunteers wore black and it was unnecessary to visibly differentiate the party members from the general population. Moreover, he believed their opponents would compare them with fascists.[50] Anna, the conciliator, saw the need to move the party to the mainstream, while Periyar, the iconoclast, was uncompromising in his ideals.

Their difference of opinion spilled over to their followers within the party. Some of the younger members who considered Anna their mentor, refused to wear black. When other members tried to bring Anna into line, he complained that a 'convention' (of wearing black) had been made into a 'compulsion'.

Periyar tried to put Anna in a dilemma by putting him in charge of a black shirts conference in Madurai. Anna avoided open confrontation by showing up at the conference wearing a black shirt himself. But when he got a chance to speak, he expressed his displeasure saying no one should be forced to wear black against their wishes. A livid Periyar called Anna a 'kulla nari' (cunning fox) for disagreeing with him.

Next, the two men clashed over a campaign to collect donations for the poet Bharathidasan[51] who was in financial difficulties. Periyar did not have great regard for litterateurs and artists. He felt donating money to a poet instead of using it for the party was a colossal waste. But Anna defied him and organized the campaign successfully. This, too, added to the animosity between the two.

The next year and a half saw back and forth sniping between the two men. Anna, who was then in the midst of the most productive phase of his literary career, turned his sharp wit on his mentor. The short stories *Label Vendaam* (no need for a label) and *Rajapart Rangadurai* (Rangadurai who Plays the King) written by him during this time were thinly veiled barbs aimed at Periyar. Using fiction, Anna pointed out that Periyar was becoming someone beyond criticism.

Periyar, who preferred blunter language, hit back saying he was in the movement for bringing about social and political change, whereas the dissidents were in it for political power alone. By the time the date for Indian independence (15 August 1947) neared, the rift between the mentor and the protégé had spilled over from tactical to strategic issues. This became the second major bone of contention.

To Mourn or Not

Periyar viewed the independence with a mixture of trepidation and foreboding. Unlike Jinnah, he had failed to create Dravida Nadu by colonial fiat. Now, an independent nation under Congress rule was on the horizon. On 27 July, he issued an announcement titled 'The Briton-Baniya-Brahmin Contract day':

> The day they are going to celebrate as a day of self-rule and independence is nothing but the start of a new imperialism—that of North Indian business interests. The Bajajs and the Birlas[5] who had functioned as British

agents so far are going to take over the country. How can this be real self-rule? (XI: p106)

Two days earlier, Dravidar Kazhagam had announced a plan to observe 15 August as a 'day of mourning'. Periyar made plans to organize meetings to popularize secession and ordered party men not to participate in any Independence Day celebrations. On 6 August, in a second announcement, he again denounced 15 August as a day of the inking of the British-Congress contract. He felt that the non-Congress people did not benefit from such a contract. Opposition to the 'day of mourning' plan came from the Anna faction. Writing in *Dravida Nadu*, Anna explained why it was an occasion for 'joy' and not 'mourning':

> Two centuries of disgrace [colonial rule] is about to be wiped off from the subcontinent. This is a joyous occasion for Dravidians too. We should be celebrating. We have been fighting two enemies so far; one of them is leaving now. Our task is getting easier. So it is an occasion for joy, not mourning. (X: p106-117)

Anna had been impressed by the way Jinnah had carved a separate nation out of India. He had succeeded where they (Periyar and Anna) had failed because he had beaten the Congress at its own game, whereas they were blindly opposing the Congress. He wanted to move the party more into the mainstream. But Periyar prevailed in the battle of wills—most of the party toed the leader's line and observed 15 August as a day of sorrow. Having lost this round, Anna retreated to plan for the next.

Though the relationship was fast approaching breaking point, both men weren't quite ready to sever ties completely. Periyar let Anna off lightly without taking any disciplinary action against him for violating the party's decision. Throughout the latter half of 1947 and the first half of 1948, the two men continued to clash. On Periyar's next birthday, Anna paid him an underhanded compliment and hinted that it was time for Periyar to quit.

The beginning of 1948 brought a respite to the shadow war in the form of Gandhi's assassination. Periyar, who had become disillusioned with Gandhi two decades earlier, was distraught when the Mahatma was killed. In a rare display of compromise, he allowed Dravidar Kazhagam members to participate in the condolence meetings organized by the Congress. He wrote a glowing obituary for Gandhi in *Viduthalai* calling for the country to be renamed as 'Gandhi Nadu' in honour of the Mahatma.

On 1 March 1948, the Congress government of Omandur Ramasamy Reddiar suddenly banned the black shirts. Anna and his supporters felt vindicated about their earlier stance. Though Anna attended a protest meeting wearing black, the animosity between the two increased further. Periyar hit back:

> There can be only one leader for a party. It is absolutely mandatory for all others to follow him... Now you have to blindly follow what I am saying. Yes, this is a form of dictatorship. If you don't like it you are free to leave. Showing dissent from within is mischievous; it is just a way to make a name for yourselves. (XV: p98)

In response, Anna boycotted a party conference at Tuticorin held on 8 May. Periyar's supporters, like M.R. Radha[53] openly disparaged Anna in the meeting. When Anna's supporters questioned Periyar about his absence, an irritated Periyar retorted:

Why are you asking me where is X or Y. Are we running an entertainment show for M.S. Subbulakshmi and K.B. Sundarambal[54] to show up? (X: p121)

A Brief Respite

When all hopes of reconciliation seemed lost, the Congress government in Madras, once again, unwittingly did something to bring the two men together. Whenever the Dravidian movement came close to succumbing to dissent and difficulties, the Congressmen would do something profoundly stupid to rejuvenate it. This time too it was the issue of language, the issue of Hindi. Continuing its obsession with Hindi, the Congress made the language a mandatory subject from the academic year 1948–49. Periyar and Anna, who were at each other's throats barely a month ago, now stood together, united against an old foe.

Periyar formed an 'anti-Hindi Army' and named Anna its 'Dictator'. *Viduthalai* and *Dravida Nadu* started attacking the new policy. June and July went by in a whirl of protest marches, conferences and demonstrations. When Rajaji (by now the governor general of the Indian dominion)[55] visited the state in August 1947, the Dravidar Kazhagam greeted him with black flags. Periyar and Anna were arrested under Section 75 of the IPC[56] and thrown in jail. The protest continued without them and soon they were released.

Periyar was very happy with Anna's activities and it looked as if the hatchet had been buried permanently. He convened a conference at Erode on 23–24 October, where it seemed that Anna was to be anointed as the heir presumptive to the party. Anna was brought to the podium in a decorated cart drawn by a pair of oxen. Alongside the cart walked Periyar with his swaying beard and trademark walking stick. Later in his speech, he openly declared Anna as his political successor:

> It is only fair that an ageing father should hand over the responsibilities to his son and I am handing over the keys to the strong box [party] to my son [Anna]. (X: p123)

Meanwhile, the protests against Hindi continued unabated and Periyar was arrested again in December. This time, the agitation turned violent and both sides tried to find a compromise. By the end of December, the government caved in and cancelled the compulsory Hindi order. A victorious Dravidar Kazhagam announced the suspension of the agitation.

The Final Showdown

The third and final break between Periyar and Anna was over the issue of Periyar's marriage to Maniammai. Within three months of anointing Anna as his successor, Periyar demonstrated that he did not really intend to hand over the party to Anna. On 2 January 1949, he announced at a party conference in Trichy that he could not trust 'someone who accepted power'.[57]

For the next few months, all was quiet in the party—Anna was busy finding success in films and Periyar was searching for an alternative heir. On 29 March, 'Brave Heart' Azhagiri died and thus deprived Periyar of another possible alternative. Periyar was a childless widower and did not have any heir for his share of the ancestral property. His nephew, E.V.K. Sampath, was the deemed heir for the family fortune and Sampath was a solid supporter of Anna. It appeared that both Periyar's party and property would go to people he did not approve of. Periyar tried to adopt a small boy as his heir. But the adoption fell through as the boy backed out. He was now looking for someone whom he could trust—someone who would follow his dictates without question.

He chose his aide Maniammai. She was the daughter of a party loyalist named Kanagasabai. She had become Periyar's personal assistant and nurse in the early '40s. Gradually, she was given more responsibilities in the party. She was put in charge of maintaining the accounts of the party's publication division. She changed her name from 'Gandhimathi' to 'Arasiyal Mani' (political bell) which was in turn shortened to Mani. She was called Maniammai out of respect by the party faithfuls. By the late 1940s, she had gained the confidence of Periyar. He made up his mind to marry her and make her his heir.

On 14 May, when Rajaji (as governor general) visited Tiruvannamalai, Periyar met him along with Maniammai. He was seeking Rajaji's legal opinion about the marriage. News of the secret meeting leaked within weeks and created a stir within the party. Party men were surprised—for them, Rajaji was the arch-enemy and the symbol of all things rotten about Brahminism. And here was their leader meeting with the enemy in secret.

Anna's supporters were suspicious that Periyar was up to something. They started a whisper campaign in the party. Periyar muddled the situation further by making cryptic allusions to 'trust' and 'heir' at a party conference in May 1949. When Anna questioned the purpose of the meeting at a Muthamizh[58] conference in Coimbatore, Periyar replied that 'it was a personal matter' and had 'nothing to do with the party'. Finally, it was out in the open—Periyar's wedding announcement[59] was posted at the office of registrar of marriages in Chennai.

This time Periyar was forced to issue an explanation in *Viduthalai* on 19 June 1949:

I was looking for a person to whom I can entrust my party and properties. I have not found such a person so far. I am not insulting anyone when I say I have not found anyone trustworthy. Who amongst you has dedicated yourself completely for our cause and the party?—The answer is no one.

He followed it up with a longer announcement on 28 June where he officially broke the news of his planned wedding with Maniammai. A storm of protest hit the party offices. Outraged party men sent thousands of telegrams urging him to reconsider and the office phones rang non-stop. Some of the party leaders like Bharathidasan, K. Anbazhagan, N.V. Natarajan, M. Karunanidhi and T.K. Sreenivasan publicly condemned the wedding plans. To get away from the bedlam, Periyar departed for Yercaud.

Anna's faction met at Chennai to consider their next course of action. Periyar was directly accusing them of disloyalty. Some amongst them counselled restraint and decided to send a delegation comprising K.K. Neelamegam, Kuthoosi Gurusamy and others to try and convince Periyar to see reason. Periyar rebuffed them saying they had no right to interfere in his personal life. A second official delegation of Dravidar Kazhagam office bearers like T.M. Parthasarathi, Kanchi Manimozhi, K.M. Kannabiran and C.V. Rajan met with the same fate. 'They will shout for four days,' said Periyar dismissing them, 'then it will be business as usual.'

On 3 July, Anna hit back with a withering article in *Dravida Nadu*. Titling it 'Periyar's Berlin Journey'[60] Anna lashed at Periyar with a fury never seen before. The inappropriateness of an old man marrying a young woman, the hypocrisy of a women's rights campaigner taking a young woman for his wife, the betrayal of loyal party volunteers by not trusting them with the party's future, seeking secret counsel from the arch enemy (Rajaji), the unilateral decision-making—all slights imagined and real were in that article. Anna had declared open war on his mentor.

Dravida Nadu carried condemnations from party men under the title 'Kanneer Thuligal' (Teardrops).[61] The party was split down the middle. Periyar tried to calm people down on 7 July, saying it was more of an adoption than a wedding. In those days, a man could not legally adopt a woman, but if he married her, then she would automatically become his heir. If Periyar had desired so, he could have thwarted the charge that he was listening to Rajaji's advice—Rajaji had in fact counselled him against marrying Maniammai. When his followers urged him to release his correspondence with Rajaji to silence Anna's criticism, he refused saying that he could not use private letters for party issues.

The wedding took place on 9 July 1949 and from there things got ugly. On 10 July, the Anna faction convened a meeting of the party's administrative committee—they were gauging the depth of discontent in the party. The response they got (32 of the 46 committee members showed up) encouraged them to split the party.

An enraged Periyar accused his opponents of planning to murder him and seize control of the party. Anna and Sampath promptly sued him for libel. They withdrew their cases only when Periyar appeared in court and clarified that he had not referred to them.

Anna gained strength as more party men started crossing over to his side. Even *Viduthalai* refused to publish Periyar's 'List of Conspirators'. The schism was final. Only the details were left to be worked out. In September, Anna announced the formation of a new party—Dravida Munnetra Kazhagam (DMK). Though they had parted ways with bitterness, Anna promised that they will always remain true to Periyar's ideals. Periyar was not impressed and remarked to his remaining associates:

> Jeevanandam left [me], Sami Chidambaranar left, Kovai Ayyamuthu left, Ponnambalanar too left. What has happened to K.M. Balasubramaniam who left me? I am not reduced because of all these desertions. Let this Annadurai go too. (X: p150)

8
Strangers in a Strange Republic

Is India a single country? Absolutely not! What we have is just a collection of various castes, religions and languages.
—Periyar on India, May 1930 (XIV: p122)

Anna was gone. The Dravidar Kazhagam had suffered its first major split. Moreover, it found itself in a completely new political environment—that of the Indian republic. Under the colonial rule, the Justice Party and the Dravidian movement had become accustomed to dealing directly with the British governor of Madras. When the British left, they also took with them the system the Justicites had become accustomed to operate within.

In the new Indian republic, the corridors of power lay in a distant and unfamiliar Delhi. To make things worse, access to that power was completely in the hands of the detested rivals—the Congressmen; and the new masters of India did not care much about the diversity of the country. The debates in the Constituent Assembly about choosing a national language for the country revealed the depths of the insensitivity of Hindi politicians to the concerns of Indians who spoke a language other than theirs.

First Blood

Unsurprisingly, Periyar did not like the new republic at all. When it was first proclaimed on 26 January 1950, he observed it as a day of mourning for Tamils. He believed it was just a change of masters; Tamils were swapping white men for local swadeshi masters and British imperialism for the North Indian variety. As if to prove his prediction true, the Communal Government Order (GO), which provided reservation for non-Brahmins in education and jobs, was struck down by the courts.

The Communal GO was first issued in 1921 during the first Justice Party government. Its provisions were implemented during the term of P. Subbarayan's independent ministry in 1927. Periyar, who had left the Congress over the issue of communal representation was a huge supporter of the reservation policy. But the GO had been passed under colonial law and not under those of the new republic. When the new republic was proclaimed, Brahmins immediately started a campaign to declare the Communal GO null and void as it violated the Articles of the Indian Constitution pertaining to equality.

The campaign started by the Salem Brahmin Welfare Association was given good publicity by the Brahmin-owned press. They challenged the legality of the GO in the Madras High Court.[62] The case was filed in April 1950 by two Brahmin students—Champakam Dorairajan and C.R. Srinivasan. Champakam claimed that the practice of allotting seats in

Madras Medical College on the basis of caste violated Article 226 of the Constitution. On 28 July, the court favoured the plaintiffs and struck down the Communal GO.

Periyar was outraged. He felt that the hard-earned victories of the last twenty years were going down the drain because of the new constitution. He organized protests condemning the court judgement and announced the observation of a 'Communal Rights Day' on 14 August. The Dravidar Kazhagam conducted meetings and conferences to protest the loss of reservations. The protesters shouted slogans like 'Down with the Constitution' and 'We want communal rights'. Thus began the first Dravidar Kazhagam agitation in the Indian republic. Soon the cause of reservation was taken up by others and the demand for a constitutional amendment to restore the GO became louder. On 27 August 1950, the Supreme Court upheld the verdict and the support for the constitutional amendment grew stronger.

In December 1950, Periyar organized a communal rights conference at Trichy. Ministers of the central government visiting Tamil Nadu were met with black flag demonstrations. At first, the central government refused to accept even a resolution passed by the Madras Legislative Assembly. Then, the Union Home Minister, Sardar Patel, visited Madras to mollify the agitators and promised action soon. On 18 June 1951, the constitutional amendment was passed and the communal GO was restored.

Periyar's first political agitation in the Indian republic ended with a success. But he was not as successful in his effort to stop the encroachment of Hindi in Tamil Nadu. When the 'Hindi wallahs' failed in their bid to make Hindi the sole national and official language of the country, they switched to a slow and incremental approach. The use of Hindi in official transactions was increased gradually so as not to provoke outright opposition.[63]

In June 1951, Hindi became a compulsory subject in inter-departmental government examinations and a Hindi Siksha Samiti (Hindi Education Committee) was set up under the central Ministry of Education to propagate the language. In 1952, a five year plan costing seventeen lakh rupees was drawn up to popularize and propagate Hindi in South India. The zeal of Hindi proponents alarmed even Rajaji, who had introduced compulsory Hindi in Tamil Nadu only fourteen years earlier. The Congress party in the state appeared to be siding with the Hindi proponents. The Dravidar Kazhagam and the DMK were opposed to introduction of Hindi in any form.

Periyar tried to mobilize anti-Hindi forces by starting an agitation to erase the Hindi letters in the name boards of government organizations. For three consecutive years beginning from the first day of August in 1952, Dravidar Kazhagam volunteers courted arrest by tarring Hindi letters on railway station and post office name boards. The DMK, too, organized similar protests. But the politicians of North India were dismissive of their concerns.[64] These initial protests did not succeed in deterring the propagation of Hindi but the language issue would lead to a bigger confrontation a decade later.

An Unintended Consequence

The first elections for the Madras State[65] under the new constitution were round the corner. The election, for the first time, was based on universal adult suffrage—people over the age of twenty-one had the right to vote. And everyone was curious about whom Periyar and Anna would support. The Dravidar Kazhagam (DK) had an announced policy of non-participation in the elections. But would the protégé follow his master in this regard? As it turned out, both chose similar yet different courses of action. Periyar chose to support communists. The Communist Party of India (CPI) had recently joined the political mainstream after an unsuccessful attempt to overthrow the Indian government through armed struggle.[66]

The Congress, after six years in power at the centre, had been weakened by factional feuds and splits. Periyar believed that the communists had the best chance to defeat the Congress. He was attracted to the communist ideals once again. He even started a Dravida Farm Labourers Union to mobilize peasants under the Dravida Nadu banner. But the alliance with communists was a troubled one from the beginning. The interests and ideals of the two parties were very different. While the communists complained that Periyar was not sympathetic enough to the class struggle, they also dismissed his Dravida Nadu demand as unattainable.

The new relationship which began in November 1951 saw lots of ups and downs. DK's executive council met and declared that defeating the Congress at any cost was its goal for the new elections. Periyar went even as far as to suggest that the DK would merge with the communists soon. But the communists were not fully comfortable with the idea of allying with Periyar. A few Brahmin communist leaders like S.A. Dange justified the anti-Brahminism of the DK saying that in South India, agrarian revolt was anti-Brahmin in nature. But others were not so sure of the alliance. In turn, Periyar was maddened by what he saw as plots of Brahminical elements within the CPI.[67] In the end, they had to settle for a partial alliance—Dravidar Kazhagam would support 16 of the 50 communist candidates in the Tamil-speaking areas of the state.

Meanwhile, Anna's Dravida Munnetra Kazhagam (DMK)

had gone along a different route. It too decided not to participate in the elections directly. Instead, it announced its support for any candidate who signed a pledge to support Dravida Nadu and raise the issue in the assembly. Two Vanniyar caste-based parties—Commonweal Party of M.A. Manickavelu Naicker and the Tamil Nadu Toilers Party of S.S. Ramasamy Padayachi, took up its offer and signed the pledge. Five other independent candidates in the northern districts also earned DMK's endorsement in the same way. Periyar was amused by Anna's political naiveté and commented in the December 1952 issue of *Viduthalai*:

> Giving support in exchange for a pledge is absurd. What surety does the DMK have that their candidates will honour that pledge? And what can he [Anna] do if they break their word?

The election held in January 1952 produced a thoroughly fractured verdict. The single largest party—Congress—won only 152 of the total 375 seats and fell short of a majority. Though it won a handy majority in the Tamil and Kannada speaking areas of the state, it was trounced by the communists in the Malabar and Andhra areas. The communists and independents emerged as the next biggest contingents in the assembly with 60 odd seats each. It was a demonstration of Periyar's political clout—of the 16 communist candidates he had supported, 13 won; but of the 34 he hadn't, only 2 made it to the assembly. But there was nothing to celebrate in the modest victory, for it led to the very last man Periyar wanted to see in power—his old rival Rajaji as the chief minister!

When it became clear that no one had won an outright majority in Madras, the opposition parties met in March 1952 and tried to form an anti-Congress coalition. The communists agreed to have T. Prakasam[68] (a former Congress chief minister who had crushed the Telengana rebellion ruthlessly) as the leader of the new coalition. Calling itself the 'United Democratic Front', the motley collection of anti-Congress parties claimed the support of 160 odd members in the assembly. Prakasam wrote to the governor staking his claim to form the government.

The Congress party was in a bind—they could not let communists come to power. In desperation, they turned to Rajaji, who by then was cooling his heels in bitter retirement.[69] Governor Sri Prakasa invited Rajaji to form the government ignoring the claims of Prakasam and gave him ample time to prove his majority in the assembly.

The man the DMK would later call a 'fox' and 'Machiavelli', set about to prove his majority with great deviousness. Rajaji was sworn in as chief minister on 14 April and proved his majority on 6 July. During the intervening three months, he had split parties, broken apart coalitions, lured independents and eventually won the confidence motion by gathering the support of 200 members![70] What was worse was that he did not even contest a by-election—he got into the legislature by getting nominated to the Legislative Council (upper house) by the governor.[71]

Periyar was aghast—he did not expect his support to the communists to backfire in such a way. If he had not supported them, the Congress would have obtained a majority of its own and Rajaji would not have gotten a new lease of political life.

Battling Hereditary Education

However, similar to events in 1937, Rajaji proved to be his own undoing. He had an authoritarian streak which made him obstinate. Some of his policies were highly unpopular with the people he governed. He had tried to impose Hindi during his previous stint as chief minister and given the Dravidar Kazhagam an issue to score over him. He repeated the same mistake now trying to implement a controversial elementary education scheme.

The new scheme proposed splitting the school day into two sessions. In the forenoon session, students would be taught at school and in the afternoon sessions, they would be sent home to learn the vocation of their parents. The scheme was controversial from the beginning. Periyar and DMK dubbed the scheme as Kula Kalvi Thittam—Hereditary Education Policy[71] and accused Rajaji of trying to perpetuate the caste hierarchy. Rajaji first announced the scheme in April 1953 and by May, the DK and the DMK had started a full-blown campaign to discredit it. Periyar thundered in *Viduthalai*:

> This educational policy is a casteist educational policy. This has to be opposed and abolished. Is this educational scheme not a reconstruction and protection of Varnashrama? Who physically labours and slaves in the name of caste? Only we, who are called Sudras... should we keep doing the caste occupation while Brahmins alone get positions, employment, authority and go higher and higher? We don't think physical labour is disgraceful, but why should we alone do that work? What is it for? Only to save his [Rajaji] race, only for the protection of the Brahmin society. As long as he is in power, he wants to fill up Brahmins in all the places. (IX: p262)

Their campaign elicited a counter campaign from the government. Rajaji and his education minister, M.V. Krishna Rao made broadcasts in All India Radio defending the scheme.

But public opinion soon turned against it. On 27 May 1953 (Buddha Purnima), Periyar suddenly announced that the Dravidar Kazhagam would break idols of Pillaiyar (Ganesh) for eradicating superstitions and to spread awareness among the people. Hundreds of Dravidar Kazhagam volunteers broke clay idols of Pillaiyar in Brahmin majority areas of the state shouting slogans like 'Long Live Buddhism' and 'Down with idol worship'. This protest distracted Periyar and the DK from the popular Kula Kalvi protest. The DMK, which refused to cooperate with the 'idol breaking protest' saying, 'We will neither break Pillaiyars nor break coconuts for him', did not waver from the Kula Kalvi protest.

The scheme came into effect in mid-June and in July the DMK announced an agitation[73] to counter it. They created a ruckus in the form of protests and picketing, to make sure that the legislature took up the issue for discussion. The assembly voted to suspend the scheme and referred it to a panel of educational experts. The July protests and the subsequent arrest and trial of the 'big five'[74] DMK leaders for their part in the agitation catapulted DMK into the limelight. Periyar was not amused. Prior to the Kula Kalvi agitation, his former protégés had been tagging along with the Dravidar Kazhagam in the anti-Hindi campaign and other protests. But when he had taken his eyes off the Kula Kalvi agitation, they had moved swiftly to occupy the vacuum.

But the scheme was not revoked completely—it was merely suspended. Periyar tried to regain the lead in opposing the scheme. He complained that his former disciples were not cooperating with him for launching a joint protest against the scheme, but he did not drop the 'idol destruction protest'. In October, he threatened to extend the protest by breaking Ram idols. When Dravidar Kazhagam volunteers received death threats, he advised them to arm themselves.

Meanwhile, public opinion had turned against the scheme completely and the Congress legislators were becoming jittery about being associated with it. On 1 October 1953, Andhra state was formed out of Madras State and the strength of the assembly was reduced to 231 from 375. The Congress had an easy majority in the rump assembly; but most of the legislators were supporters of the Congress leader Kamaraj.[75] Rajaji's position within the party became precarious.

In November, the expert Parulekar committee (set up earlier by the state government due to pressure from the opposition parties) endorsed the scheme completely and recommended its implementation from the next academic year. But the Congress lost a by-election in November and the party men could clearly see the public disenchantment with the scheme. They began to manoeuvre Rajaji out of power. He managed to hang on till March 1954, when he finally resigned to avoid a humiliating defeat in party leadership polls.

Kamaraj, who succeeded Rajaji as Congress chief minister in April, was opposed to the controversial scheme. He made the education minister C. Subramaniam (who ironically had been among the scheme's original architects) drop it citing public opposition. Periyar was elated. Thirty years after he had walked out of the Congress, the party had done something he wholeheartedly agreed with. He welcomed Kamaraj's taking over the reigns as a boon for the Dravidian cause. Thus began the long and uneasy alliance between the two men.

9
An Uneasy Alliance

There is a wrong impression that there is an understanding between the Congress in Tamil Nadu and Mr Naicker. Let me at once make it clear that the Congress organisation has no understanding at all with him.
—Kamaraj, denying any formal alliance between Congress and Periyar, February 1962 (XXI: 214)

When Periyar started the Self-Respect Movement in 1925, one of its stated goals was to destroy the Congress. For thirty years he had done his best to accomplish the goal. Thus, it was a strange sight when he started to campaign for a Congress candidate in the Gudiyatham by-election in August 1954. The candidate was none other than the new chief minister Kamaraj. Periyar explained his decision to support the Congress thus:

Since Mr Kamaraj has done his best to serve the Tamils, since he has changed Acharyar's [Rajaji] educational system designed to perpetuate the caste system, since he has conferred many jobs and many benefits on Tamils in the educational and other spheres and since the Brahmins and the DMK are trying to oust him from power, it has become the duty of all Tamils to support Mr. Kamaraj and his followers in the election. (*The Hindu*, 10 October 1956)

Periyar believed it was the first time a Tamil had become chief minister of the state and good things would come out of it.[76] Once he threw his support behind Kamaraj, Anna and the DMK were also forced to acknowledge the 'goodness' of Kamaraj and support him themselves. Only the communists were left to oppose him.

Kamaraj had an easy victory in the election. But many in the Congress were not happy with their newfound ally. By December 1954, the muttering within the party became strong enough to force Kamaraj to issue a disclaimer. He denied that the Congress was becoming closer to the Dravidar Kazhagam or adopting its ideologies. This uneasy situation continued over the next decade—Periyar would openly support Kamaraj and Congress; they in return would welcome the support privately but denounce it publicly.

Dravida Nadu to Tamil Nadu

1954 saw the last of the Dravidar Kazhagam's serious agitations against Hindi. For the previous three years, on the first day of August, they had been tarring Hindi letters on the name boards of government offices as a protest against encroachment of Hindi into Tamil Nadu. Kamaraj was sympathetic to their cause. When Periyar was away on a trip to Malaysia, Kamaraj made a speech at a meeting organized by the Vanniyar caste association, in which he supported the non-Brahmin ideology of the Dravidar Kazhagam. It was a vindication of sorts for Periyar's support to him.

In 1955, Periyar announced a change in plans for the party's usual anti-Hindi protests scheduled for 1 August ; they would not be tarring the Hindi letters, instead they would be burning the Indian National Flag. This announcement sent shock waves throughout the state. M. Bhaktavatsalam, the state's agriculture minister, warned Periyar on 24 July that the flag burners would be severely dealt with. Periyar dared him to do what he could. Although many people found the notion of flag burning deeply offensive, there was no specific law prohibiting it.

On 29 July, Kamaraj assured Periyar that he would not permit Hindi imposition in the state. Periyar was happy—it was the first time someone in power had explicitly opposed Hindi. In return, he cancelled the planned flag-burning agitation. It would be the last time Dravidar Kazhagam held any serious agitations against Hindi—Periyar was content with Kamaraj's promise on the issue.

Periyar's attention soon shifted to the reorganization of states. For some time, the idea of forming states on linguistic basis had been gaining ground. The communists were vocal supporters of linguistic states. In October 1955, a States Reorganization Commission (SRC) was formed under Justice Fazal Ali to draw up the boundaries for new states. There was intense competition among the new states to gain as much territory as possible for themselves. Several border regions became contested as more than one state claimed them.

Kerala and Tamil Nadu were embroiled in one such dispute over Devikulam, Peermedu and Kanyakumari district. In a rare display of unity, Congress, DK and DMK came together with a demand that those regions be retained within the Madras State. However, despite their efforts, Devikulam and Peermedu (currently in Idukki district) were awarded to Kerala.

The Congress made one last effort to stop the formation of linguistic states. P.C. Roy, West Bengal's Congress chief minister proposed an alternate plan to set up large states. Under his plan, most of South India would be united into a single province called Dakshin Pradesh (Southern Province). Rajaji and Kamaraj supported the idea while Periyar and Anna opposed it. Periyar, who had once demanded a Dravida Nadu with nearly identical boundaries, was now opposed to such an entity.[77] He believed that in such a state, Tamils would be a minority and discriminated against. It was during this period that the Dravidar Kazhagam's Dravida Nadu demand morphed into the 'Tamil Nadu' demand.

The Dakshin Pradesh idea was formally accepted by the All India Congress Committee in Februay 1956. Kamaraj was supportive of the idea initially. The chief ministers of Kerala and Karnataka were also receptive to it. But when the Congress executive committee met at Bangalore, Periyar sent Kamaraj a telegram urging him to oppose the idea. Subsequently, Kamaraj changed his mind and opposed it. Without his support, the Dakshin Pradesh proposal had to be abandoned.

Rise of the DMK

While Periyar was becoming closer to Kamaraj, Anna and DMK were silently filling up the opposition vacuum in the state. After the communist strongholds—Andhra and Malabar—split from Madras State in 1953, the Madras Communist Party was a pale imitation of its former self. In May 1957, the DMK held an internal referendum at their party conference in Salem over participating in elections. An overwhelming majority of the party cadres voted for contesting the next years' elections. To thwart Periyar's criticism about his hunger for power, Anna cleverly used the referendum to justify the decision as the 'will of the party'.

With the DMK directly entering the electoral fray, Kamaraj and Periyar needed each other more than ever. A number of known DK sympathizers in the Congress were among the party's candidates for the elections. Periyar's support for the Congress caused a split in its ranks. Rajaji, still smarting from his earlier ouster by Kamaraj, convinced a small section of the Congressmen opposed to the Dravidar Kazhagam to quit the party. They formed a new party called Congress Reform Committee (CRC) and contested the elections. Periyar campaigned for the Congress and reserved his strongest attacks for his former disciples. He even campaigned for Anna's opponent in Kanchipuram constituency (ironically a Brahmin).

The election, held in March 1956, resulted in Kamaraj returning as chief minister easily. The split of the opposition votes between the DMK, CRC and the communists made sure Congress won an unassailable majority in the new assembly. Though Anna and fourteen other DMK candidates won their contests, Periyar was satisfied with Kamaraj's return to power.

Snakes and Brahmins

While the DMK was preparing to join the mainstream, Periyar was busy fighting caste wars. Sidelining the Hindi issue, he took up caste in its place. He renewed his campaign against Ram and Ramayana in August 1956. He declared that Ram and Sita were not Tamil gods and burnt their effigies. He was arrested along with a thousand other volunteers of the Dravidar

Kazhagam and booked under Section 295 of the IPC. Later persuaded by Kamaraj, he suspended the agitation.

Once the 1957 elections were over, he started the anti-caste campaign once again, this time specifically targetting Brahmins. In those days it was common to see exclusive 'Brahmin coffee clubs' and 'Brahmin hotels' in the state. They had a separate dining area for the Brahmins. Periyar announced a campaign against this practice and organized picketing of the establishments catering exclusively to Brahmins.[79] Dravidar Kazhagam volunteers tarred the word 'Brahmin' in the name boards of those establishments. But the Kamaraj government refused to ban such hotels and Periyar was only partially successful in raising awareness about the discriminative practice.

Having failed in his attempt to ban Brahmin hotels, he ratcheted up his campaign a bit. He declared the tuft and the punool (sacred thread) worn by the Brahmins as a symbol of high caste oppression and announced his intention to cut them off. Explaining the reason behind the campaign, at a public meeting in Chidambaram on 9 July 1957, he said:

> The First step towards abolition of caste would be to give up marks that indicate one's caste. The idea of superiority or inferiority by birth should be eliminated from the minds of the people. If needed, a stiffer campaign with more radical methods will be adopted to achieve this. It doesn't matter if a few thousand of us are imprisoned or sent to gallows. Such sacrifices are worth making if the next generation can be freed from the evils of the caste system. (XXII: p83)

But he did not include the other castes which wore the sacred thread in his target list—only Brahmins were singled out for the rough treatment. When the Congressmen threatened to ban the Dravidar Kazhagam, he retorted that they would break statues of Gandhi all over the state.

Soon the campaign turned ugly with frequent incidents of violence against Brahmins. Dravidar Kazhagam members forcibly cut off the tufts and sacred threads of a few Brahmins and it created a nationwide outrage. In retaliation, they were attacked in some places. Slogans like 'If you see a Brahmin and a snake at the same time, kill the Brahmin first, for he is more venomous' were used by DK men to incite hatred against Brahmins.

With mounting pressure to take action, Kamaraj had Periyar arrested and convicted for making 'objectionable speeches'. Though he was granted bail quickly, the violence escalated. When he came out of prison, he announced the burning of the *Manusmriti* and parts of the Indian Constitution to protest the 'promotion of caste' by the Indian state. In those days, there were no specific laws banning the burning of the Constitution. In response to his announcement, the Kamaraj government hurriedly passed a special law—The Prevention of Insults to National Honour Act—to ban the practice.

In November 1957, Periyar went ahead and burnt the Constitution. He was arrested along with ten thousand party volunteers and convicted under the new law. When he was in jail, there was a sudden increase in violence against Brahmins. After a Brahmin public prosecutor (who had conducted the case against Periyar) was attacked by angry party men, Periyar was forced to appeal to them to remain calm. Realizing that things were getting out of control, he suspended the agitation in December 1957.

1957 was the high tide of the anti-Brahmin campaign of the Dravidar Kazhagam. It was becoming increasingly ineffective—with a non-Brahmin chief minister in power, the spectre of

Brahmin oppression was not as potent as it had been earlier. Calls for social boycott of Brahmins went nowhere. For the better part of the next decade, the Dravidar Kazhagam soft pedalled on the anti-Brahmin issue and shifted its focus to defeating the DMK instead. While Periyar had been preoccupied with Brahmins and caste, the DMK had been slowly positioning itself as a moderate alternative to the Dravidar Kazhagam.

A Political Suicide

The late 1950s and the early 1960s were a little bit subdued and uneventful for Periyar and Dravidar Kazhagam. He was eighty years old and his health was failing fast. Nearly forty years of gruelling public life had taken its toll. He had to restrict his public appearances. To lighten his schedule, he hit upon a novel scheme—he started charging for his appointments. Party members and ideological followers had to donate money to the party to meet him, to get photographed with him or to have him appear in their family functions. This way he was able to keep the party finances unaffected while reducing his workload.

Periyar briefly revived the anti-Hindi agitation in 1960. DK volunteers burnt Indian maps in public and courted arrest. But the agitation did not capture the public imagination—by then the DMK had taken over the lead in the language issue.

When the next election came along in 1962, the DMK emerged as the principal opposition to the Congress in the state. Winning a series of local body elections, it became a formidable political force. The DMK and Communists led the attack on Kamaraj from the political left on economic and social issues.

Rajaji had converted the CRC into a full-fledged political party called the Swatantara Party in October 1959 and launched an offensive on the Congress from the right. Periyar saw the danger the Congress faced and extended his unconditional support to Kamaraj. In the November 1961 issue of *Viduthalai*, Periyar announced that DK would work for Congress candidates, even if they fielded pieces of clay or wood. The only thing that mattered was keeping Kamaraj in power.

Periyar was particularly worried about an alliance between the 'teardrops' (DMK) and the 'fake currency party' (Swatantara).[80] Fortunately for him, the differences between the opposition proved too wide to be bridged in time and they remained disunited.

Despite his age and feeble condition, Periyar hit the road campaigning non-stop for Congress candidates. He detailed the achievements of Kamaraj and disparaged Anna and his wers as irresponsible spendthrifts. *Viduthalai* carried articles extolling the virtues of the Kamaraj government. But his spirited campaign caused headaches for Kamaraj. When Periyar issued a warning to Brahmin voters not to go near polling booths on Election Day, he was severely condemned and criticised all around. Kamaraj was forced to deny that there was any understanding between him and Periyar. But despite these hiccups Periyar campaigned himself to exhaustion.

When the results came in, Periyar was recuperating in a hospital. Congress had returned to power, but with a reduced majority. Anna had lost in Kanchipuram, but DMK's tally was thrice the number they had won last time. It was clear that the opposition's disunity had cost them dearly.

But Kamaraj did not stay on as Chief Minister for long. To rejuvenate a stagnant Congress party in the states and the centre, he developed what was later dubbed as the 'Kamaraj plan' or the 'K plan'. It called for Congress leaders who had been in power for long to resign and take up party posts instead. This way they would make way for the next generation of Congress leaders and also spend time trying to rebuild the party organization. Kamaraj himself took the lead and resigned as chief minister of Madras State in October 1963. He left for Delhi to take up the post of the All India Congress Committee Secretary. A number of senior leaders like Morarji Desai, Jagjivan Ram, Lal Bahadur Shastri and Biju Patnaik followed his lead and resigned from their government positions. Periyar was horrified by this development. He sent a telegram to Kamaraj imploring him to change his mind:

> Either of your own accord or on advice of others, your resignation of the Chief Ministership will be suicidal to Tamils, Tamil Nadu and yourself. (XXII: p215)

Kamaraj did not change his mind and Periyar's words proved prophetic. The man who succeeded Kamaraj as chief minister was M. Bhaktavatasalam—an unimaginative and unpopular leader. He lacked both the 'charisma and the political acumen' of Kamaraj. His tenure as chief minister was a boon to the DMK.

In the 1960s, India experienced an acute food shortage, which led to a severe rise in prices of essential commodities.[81] DMK capitalised on the inept handling of the food crisis by the state administration.

Slogans like 'Bhaktavatsalam annachi arisi vilai ennachu?'— Big brother Bhaktavatasalam, why is the price of rice so high? 'Kamaraj Annachi kadalai paruppu vilai ennachu?'—Big brother Kamaraj what happened to the price of pulses? were used by the DMK to portray the helplessness of the Congress administration.

Kamaraj, now at a distant Delhi, could only watch, as Bhaktavatsalam squandered the goodwill he had accumulated over the past decade. The second anti-Hindi agitation organized by the DMK in 1965 was the final nail in the coffin for the

Bhaktavatsalam government. Bhaktavatsalam's brutal tactics in crushing the agitators using paramilitary forces and the high number of lives lost turned a majority of voters against the Congress. The opposition parties united under Anna's leadership to take on the Congress.[82] In the next elections in 1967, Congress was left without any allies other than Periyar. Even his spirited campaign could not save Kamaraj and the Congress from a crushing defeat. It was a dual blow for Periyar—Kamaraj was defeated and the 'teardrops' had triumphed with the help of Rajaji.

10
Enemies to Friends

> *Annadurai is a very talented man. Soon he will be free from the clutches of the Rajaji cabal. There might come a time, when we will welcome his return to power.*
> —Periyar welcoming Anna's accession to power, 1967 (XIV: p105)

Periyar had a love-hate relationship with the DMK. For a long time, he could not forgive Anna for splitting the Dravidian movement. He took special care to try and curtail the growth of the DMK whenever possible. But the relationship was not one of simple hatred—there were a few acts of goodwill sprinkled amongst a decade and half of hostility.

The DMK did not have a party president—it kept the post vacant out of respect for Periyar; they said they considered him to be their leader. Within a year of the momentous split, the former mentor and protégé found themselves occupying adjacent cells in the Trichy jail. Both were there for similar reasons—writing incendiary books.

Periyar's crime was publishing *Periyarin Ponmozhigal* (The Sayings of Periyar), while Anna's was writing *Arya Mayai* (The Aryan Myth). Both books were accused of inciting hatred and were banned. Periyar and Anna were fined heftily and both chose prison instead of paying their fines. For ten days, they sat in their cells without talking to each other. On the eleventh day, they were granted bail. When he came out of prison in 1950, Periyar found a huge crowd waiting to receive him. He was puzzled—those were not his party men; they were DMK members. He realized that it was the handiwork of Anna. This broke the ice—to the amazement of their followers, the rivals left in the same car like nothing had changed between them.

In the early '50s, the Dravidar Kazhagam was the dominant force in the Dravidian movement. The upstart DMK had to attach itself to DK's agitations. During the first amendment/ communal rights agitation, DMK joined Periyar in his campaign for restoring caste-based reservation. In August 1950, it even participated in a procession led by Periyar from Broadway in Madras. Anna announced that with respect to social issues, the DK and the DMK were like a double-barrelled gun. It was only in 1953 that the DMK started going on its own path. Periyar's closeness to Kamaraj was growing and the DMK had to find its own political space for survival.

DK vs DMK

From 1953 to '67, Periyar opposed Anna tooth and nail. Except for a few occasions, the DK and DMK found themselves at opposite sides in all issues. DMK's decision to participate in the 1957 election was strongly criticized by Periyar. It was a vindication of sorts for his earlier allegations that Anna was power-hungry. To counter his criticism, Anna had to orchestrate an elaborate intra-party campaign for giving legitimacy to the decision. But Periyar was not convinced. He took special care to campaign against DMK candidates in the 1957 election. A large number of Periyar supporters were fielded as Congress candidates in the election. This became the first direct confrontation between the two Dravidian parties. It ended in a draw—though the DK-supported Congress won an easy majority, the DMK was able to open its account in the state legislature. An incensed Periyar denounced Anna in the March 1957 issue of *Viduthalai*:

> Winning fifteen seats and entering the legislature cannot eradicate caste. Those who change their name to 'Annadurai Mudaliar' to contest in elections will not do anything to eradicate caste. They will say anything to win a few more seats. Thankfully I am alive today—had I been dead, the teardrops [DMK] would have used my death to garner sympathy and win a hundred seats. (XV: p127)

As the DMK grew with every election, winning more and more votes, the bitterness intensified. In the next assembly elections in 1962, Periyar took special care to target the incumbent DMK MLAs. The Dravidar Kazhagam campaigned against them with extra zeal. Of the fifteen DMK members who had won in 1957, fourteen lost in 1962. Only Karunanidhi escaped defeat in the Kulithalai constituency, despite a special cycle wing of the Dravidar Kazhagam giving extra attention to Kulithalai. Even Anna lost his seat to a novice Congress candidate. A miffed Anna took off to Bangalore to sulk.

While concentrating on the DMK incumbents, Periyar and Kamaraj had failed to check DMK's growth elsewhere—its strength in the new assembly grew to fifty. Kamaraj's resignation as chief minister in 1963 was an unexpected windfall for the DMK. His successor Bhaktavatsalam bungled the handling of several issues and support for the Congress eroded away.

In 1965, the official language issue flared into the second major anti-Hindi agitation. This time, Periyar was firmly on the side of the government. He deplored the agitations turning violent and held the DMK responsible for inciting students. He urged the Congress government to deal with the agitators more harshly and close down the newspapers carrying inflammatory articles. He wanted the state government to announce its stance on Hindi clearly to end the speculation on the language issue. He still believed Kamaraj could deliver on his earlier promise to stop the imposition of Hindi.

Unfortunately for him, the Hindi fanatics in the central government did not heed Kamaraj's warnings and were intent on making it the sole official language of the nation. When the violence subsided after Anna's appeal to the students, Periyar believed it to be the proof of the DMK being behind the violence. The agitation ended as a victory for the DMK—the central government backtracked and assured Tamils that the status quo would be preserved; English would continue as an official language.

The image of the Congress was completely tarnished in the eyes of the people. In the next election in 1967, the opposition fielded a unified grand alliance against the Congress. The communists joined the DMK and the right wing Swatantara to form a truly rainbow alliance. At the height of the campaign, DMK candidate and popular actor M.G. Ramachandran (MGR) was shot and wounded by M.R. Radha, another actor with known DK sympathies. Radha then tried unsuccessfully to commit suicide and both men were hospitalized. This sensational news swept the state and added to DMK's support.

There were sporadic incidents of violence in the state and police protection had to be provided for the Congress and DK leaders. Periyar was disgusted:

> Both Radha and Ramachandran (MGR) are actors. They play all sorts of characters—however disgusting they may be. How can they be expected to have the personal integrity and honesty that is essential for public life? This [shooting] is a shameful personal incident that happened between two lowly actors. Why such a frenzy over this? People are becoming emotional over a trivial incident. Has our society degenerated so bad that the government is concerned about a quarrel between actors? Because of this incident, it is banning meetings and gatherings under section 144 [of the Indian Penal Code]... Are we living in a state ruled by an actors' government? I am frustrated because, due to such a trivial incident Congress offices have been torched, police is protecting my house and Kamaraj's house. If Kamaraj himself has to be protected then who else can be safe in this state? People have to start thinking about this situation. (XV: p135)

Despite Periyar's backing, the opposition tide swept over the Congress. DMK won an outright majority on its own and Anna became the first non-Congress chief minister of Tamil Nadu. Even Kamaraj was defeated by a student leader in the Virudhunagar constituency. A victorious Anna visited his former mentor at Trichy to get his blessings before being sworn in as chief minister. He was accompanied by his senior cabinet members—Karunanidhi and Nedunchezhiyan. Periyar was rendered speechless by this gesture of Anna. Here were his avowed enemies, asking him to be their guide and advisor in the administration of the state. He agreed to help them. In June 1967, Anna announced in the legislature that the DMK government owed everything to Periyar and by September, Periyar too publicly declared his support to Anna.

The long rift had finally healed.

The Advisor

Periyar stayed true to his word—he served as a sounding board and advisor to the new DMK government. But he did not hesitate to criticize the government when he felt they were not being true to the Dravidian ideology. There was some criticism within and outside the party that he had conveniently shifted support to those in power. As the new government had the support of DK's arch rival Rajaji, Periyar's detractors viewed this as an obvious contradiction to his earlier stance. Periyar explained that DMK and Swatantara would soon fall out:

> Annadurai is saying he is running a family. But it is a strange family—where the husband (Rajaji) is casting doubts on the conduct of the wife (DMK). This cannot go on forever. (XV: p140)

His prediction came true as Swatantara withdrew support to the DMK government after disagreeing with many of its policies. He also justified his support to the DMK by pointing out that they still remained atheists and had not invoked God's name while taking the oath of office.

Though Periyar was generally supportive of Anna's policies, there were several issues in which he differed with him. For instance, when the government attempted to make Tamil the sole medium of instruction for higher education, Periyar did not agree with them. He pointed out the advantages of learning in English. Similarly, another point of contention between Periyar and Anna was the second world Tamil conference held at Chennai in 1968. DMK, which claimed to be a patron of the Tamil language, organized the conference at a huge cost and with great fanfare. Periyar felt such an extravaganza was unnecessary for the state:

> Why do we need a conference for Tamil? Why not a conference for onions? Our improvement and welfare has nothing to do with speaking in chaste Tamil. We should use a mixture of English and Tamil while speaking. (XV: p142)

He was also impatient with Anna's government on its reluctance to impose the radical rationalist agenda over the Tamil people. As a first step toward popularizing rationalism, he demanded that all government holidays for religious festivals be banned. But Anna was reluctant to adopt such an overtly atheist agenda. Instead, he took the middle path and banned the display of pictures of Hindu gods in government offices.

Such half-hearted measures did not satisfy Periyar. He felt that the DMK had a mandate to impose rationalism and was failing to do so. Periyar also did not like the flagship programme of DMK's election manifesto—providing three measures of rice for one rupee.[83] According to him, the scheme was economically unfeasible and he urged Anna to drop it as soon as possible.

In 1968, Anna's health worsened suddenly—he was suffering from the cancer of the gullet—and he had to be flown to America for surgery. Despite the surgery, the cancer claimed his life in February 1969. Periyar was greatly saddened to lose the disciple who had bested him. He was even more dismayed by the power struggle that developed in the DMK after Anna's death. The number 2 and number 3 in Anna's cabinet—

Nedunchezhiyan and Karunanidhi—were locked in a contest for becoming his successor. A vicious faction fight developed within the party and harsh words were thrown around.

Periyar tried and failed to broker a peace deal between the two factions. Finally, Karunanidhi prevailed with the help of MGR and became the chief minister on 10 February 1969. A miffed Nedunchezhiyan refused to take up a post in his cabinet. Periyar and others counselled him and brokered a compromise. In return for accepting Karunanidhi's leadership, he was made the party's general secretary.[84]

The Guiding Light

Periyar was much friendlier to the new Karunanidhi government than he had been to Anna's. Karunanidhi was more willing to legislate some of the radical parts of the Dravidian Movement's agenda. With Rajaji severing his ties with the DMK, it became easy for Periyar to back his former disciples. He became the unofficial guiding light for the new government.

In 1970, he launched an agitation demanding people of all castes should be allowed to become priests in Hindu temples. As such there was no law preventing anyone from becoming a priest; only the weight of tradition limited priesthood to Brahmins alone. Periyar's logic was that since the tax money of non-Brahmins was being utilized to run temples, they should be allowed to become priests. As part of the agitation, he revived some aspects of his campaign against Brahmins. This time he did not call for outright social boycott of Brahmins, but initiated a limited anti-Brahmin propaganda campaign. The Dravidar Kazhagam announced that it would forcibly enter the sanctums of Hindu temples and conduct archanai (offerings) to the deities.

Realizing that such acts would cause law and order problems in the state, Karunanidhi assured Periyar that the government would take care of the issue. He amended the Hindu Religious and Endowments Act in 1970, to allow non-Brahmins to become priests in Hindu temples.[85] Accepting this solution, Periyar dropped the sanctum entry agitation.

In January 1971, Karunanidhi dissolved his cabinet and decided to seek a fresh mandate from the people. Elections for the Tamil Nadu Assembly were scheduled along with those for the Indian Parliament. This election saw a complete political realignment in the state. The Indian National Congress had split in 1969 into Indira and Organization factions.[86]

In Tamil Nadu, Kamaraj was the leader of the Congress (Organization). Most of the Tamil Nadu Congress was behind him and the Indira faction was weak in the state. For the 1971 elections, Kamaraj allied with his rival, Rajaji, to take on the DMK. Karunanidhi struck a deal with Indira Gandhi whereby the Congress (Indira) supported the DMK in the assembly elections but did not contest any seats. Periyar welcomed such a coalition. He was against the Kamaraj–Rajaji alliance. He said in the *Viduthalai* editorial dated December 1970:

> A pony and a buffalo cannot pull a cart together. A state government that can dictate to the central government and a central government that takes care of the state are essential for Tamil Nadu's welfare. DMK and Indira Congress can provide those. We have to defeat the Kamaraj–Rajaji alliance which is out to destroy such an opportunity.

With the split in Congress votes and the backing of Periyar, DMK scored a mammoth victory in the polls, winning 184 seats on its own and Karunanidhi returned as chief minister. This election was the last major one in which the old giants of Tamil Nadu politics—Kamaraj, Periyar and Rajaji would participate.

The Final Years

Even well into his nineties, Periyar kept up his rationalist campaign. His mobility was limited and he was not able to travel as frequently as he liked. But he still kept himself involved in the daily politics of Tamil Nadu. When MGR quarrelled with Karunanidhi in 1972 and split from DMK, Periyar backed the latter. MGR was the treasurer of the DMK and he had asked the party members to declare their expenses publicly. Periyar did not approve of his actions. He opined:

> A party treasurer should have asked for and got the accounts in private. He should not have done this in public. The party leadership is correct in not tolerating this and taking action against him. (XV: p148)

Periyar's support came as a shot in the arm for Karunanidhi. While he supported Karunanidhi, Periyar also realized that the loss of MGR would be a boost for the opponents of the Dravidian movement. He tried to convince MGR to stay with the party. But MGR did not listen to him—he started a new party called Anna Dravida Munnetra Kazhagam (ADMK) to oppose the DMK. Periyar was angered by his actions. 'It is Annadurai's fault,' he lamented. 'MGR is not one of us and he doesn't belong to our race. Why did Annadurai allow him to join the party? Maybe if he did not have tax problems, he would not have started a new party.'[88]

Rajaji died in December 1972. Despite his own frailty and advanced years, Periyar attended Rajaji's funeral to bid good bye to his lifelong friend and adversary. Opponents and supporters alike were taken aback to see tears in Periyar's eyes—he who had not shed a single drop for his beloved wife's death was openly crying for his arch rival.

On 23 December 1973, Periyar attended his last public meeting—organized at T Nagar to spread awareness against superstitions. He summed up the state of the Dravidian movement thus:

> When I started the Self-Respect Movement, we had five basic goals—to destroy God, Gandhi, Congress, Religion and Brahmins. Of these, Gandhi is dead; Congress too is gone. God's condition is laughable. But when we pass laws to allow anyone to become priests, they [Brahmins] get it annulled. We should change this state of affairs.

He couldn't continue beyond a few minutes. His body wasn't cooperating and he had to conclude his speech. There were tears in the eyes of his volunteers to see him in such pain. The meeting was over by ten o'clock. His condition worsened rapidly during the night and he was admitted to the Vellore Medical College hospital. He breathed his last at 7.22 a.m. the next day (24 December 1973). He was buried with full state honours.

11
The Legacy

Prophet of the New Age, the Socrates of Southeast Asia, Father of Social Reform Movement, and arch enemy of ignorance, superstitions, meaningless customs and base manners.

Citation in UNESCO award to Periyar
27 June 1970

Probably there is no other personality in the history of Tamil Nadu whose legacy has been debated and fought over as much as that of Periyar's. Nearly half a century after his death, even the issue of how to refer to him is hotly contested. His views on women, caste, Brahmins, Hinduism, Tamil, India, Congress, Gandhi, DMK—all are fodder for bickering today. The Dravidian parties which have ruled the state continuously for the past four decades have deified him and tried to make him into a figure of veneration. However, for the followers of Hindutva, he remains a divisive figure who stoked hatred and incited violence against Brahmins. Even among Dalits, a section now challenges his depiction as a campaigner for the rights of all non-Brahmins.

The Dravidar Kazhagam, which he created out of the remains of the Justice Party, has split and the splinters are arguing over who holds the copyright to his writings. Periyar's legacy is diverse and wide-ranging.

Political legacy

The DMK became the first non-Congress state party to come to power with an absolute majority in independent India. Though Periyar was against it from the moment of its creation, it owes a great deal of its success to the ideals it borrowed from him. Periyar's ideology was not suited for electoral politics. Successful politicians have to take care not to offend too many of their constituents. However, Periyar's ideology thrived on confrontation and taking on the establishment. It took Anna's particular genius to take the core of Periyar's ideals and package it in a form acceptable to a majority of the people. But without that core, Anna would not have been able to present DMK as an alternative to the Congress.

Periyar was not an armchair revolutionary. He had a hands-on approach toward all the social and political movements he organized. He made hundreds of public appearances every year and was arrested nineteen times. He was not one to shy away from confronting those in power. Even when his health failed in his final years, he had himself wheeled to public meetings with a urine bucket in tow. He was the first person in the state to talk about social issues in the public and use political platforms to campaign for social reform. Till his advent, only nationalism was used to mobilize the masses—he proved that social issues too could be used to do that.

The Dravidian parties—the DMK and the AIADMK—that

have ruled Tamil Nadu for the past four decades, owe a lot to him. But his own party, the Dravidar Kazhagam, is a pale shadow of its former self. After Periyar's death, it was headed by his wife Maniammai briefly and since 1978 has been under the leadership of K. Veeramani. It still does not contest elections but has sided with the DMK or the AIADMK in various elections. It split in 1996, when Viduthalai Rajendran left to form the Periyar Dravidar Kazhagam. The two factions were involved in a protracted court battle over who owned the copyright to Periyar's works. Both conduct small-scale agitations for the causes they are involved in like the Sri Lankan Tamils issue, the Mullaperiyar dam issue and generally support opposing coalitions in the elections.

The Dravidar Kazhagam also runs a university—the Periyar Maniammai University—in the state. Periyar's secessionist agenda, though never renounced formally, has gradually been replaced with the goal of securing more rights for Tamil Nadu and Tamils within the Republic of India.

Social Legacy

Periyar's greatest impact on Tamil and Indian society has been through his anti-caste and reservation campaigns. The demand for communal representation first brought him into the Congress and later made him walk out of it in disgust when the party refused to agree to it. Communal representation became the backbone of the reservation policy in India. Periyar's agitation against the Supreme Court verdict de-legitimizing reservation played a part in the enactment of the First Amendment to the Indian Constitution to make it legal again. Since then, reservation in jobs and education for non-Brahmin castes has increased slowly all over India. In

Tamil Nadu, the percentage of reservation has been gradually increased over the years—currently it is at 69 per cent (though in effect it is only 50 per cent, as extra 'open category' seats were created due to a Supreme Court order issued in 1963 to restrict reservation to 50 per cent). The Mandal Commission report implementation in 1990 and the 93rd constitutional amendment in 2005 have increased quotas for non-Brahmins nationwide. Thus, a major part of Periyar's legacy is still alive in the country. The Dravidar Kazhagam is an active participant in legal actions for safeguarding these reservations.

But Periyar's goal of total eradication of caste has failed miserably, with caste divisions still deeply entrenched in Tamil Nadu. Yet, there has been some progress. For example, one of the most visible effects of Periyar's anti-caste campaign is the almost complete absence of caste-based surnames in Tamil Nadu. It is due to him that flaunting caste and justifying discrimination based on birth has become something to be frowned upon and done without fanfare. One does find caste-based discrimination in Tamil Nadu but its perpetrators lack the ability to justify it openly because the Dravidian movement's campaign has made it unfashionable.

The Self-Respect weddings introduced by Periyar never caught on with the general public. Though they were given legal recognition by Anna's government in 1968, only a few party faithfuls still use them for getting married. Inter-caste and inter-religious marriages are on the rise, but nowhere in numbers required to form a casteless, religion-less society in the foreseeable future.

Perhaps the most divisive and ugly part of Periyar's legacy is the strain of anti-Brahminism that exists in the state. Speeches delivered by him in the later part of his life (especially the anti-Brahmin movement in the 1950s) were strident against

Brahmins. Despite his venomous attacks on Brahmins, he seems to have had little personal animosity towards them (as evidenced by his friendship with prominent Brahmins like Rajaji). Periyar remains a highly hated and divisive figure for Hindu right-wing organizations like the Hindu Munnani, the RSS and other Sangh Parivar outfits in Tamil Nadu. Brahmin-controlled media outlets like *Thuglak* and *Dinamalar* and the 'internet Hindus' take pains to counter the official narrative about Periyar and minimize his accomplishments. The recent flame war between Tamil writer Jayamohan and Periyar's supporters over his role in the Vaikom Satyagraha is an excellent example of the right-wing retaliation against Periyar.

The last element of Periyar's agenda—to allow people of all castes to become priests in temples—is yet to come to fruition. Despite forty years of Dravidian rule and a couple of attempts at implementation through legislation, the Anaivarum Archgaragalaam Thittam ('All can become priests' scheme) has been stalled due to legal challenges.

Periyar's rationalist ideology has been diluted by his political heirs. In particular, the atheist plank has almost been abandoned by the Dravidian parties. The 'There is no God' policy first devolved into the 'One Race, One God' stance of Anna and later to the outright theism of the AIADMK under MGR and J. Jayalalitha. Atheism and criticism of religious rituals are no longer fashionable in Tamil politics. Among all the major Dravidian party leaders, only Karunanidhi is still openly atheistic. The campaigns against Ram and Pillaiyar have also petered out.

Periyar's call for women's rights too underwent a sea change in the hands of the Dravidian parties. Periyar called for complete equality between the sexes; he viewed chastity and obedience to husbands as archaic concepts designed to subjugate women. But his political heirs have abandoned such views and have made chastity into a mandatory quality for Tamil women. The adoption of Kannagi, the protagonist of *Silappadikaram*, the second century epic, as a symbol of Tamil womanhood is completely at odds with Periyar's vision for women. The vilification of actress Khushboo for her public comments on premarital sex and chastity in 2005 is emblematic of the subversion of Periyar's message. After all, what Khushboo said was much milder than Periyar's own writings in the 1920s and '30s.

Literary Legacy

Periyar has left behind a huge number of published works—books, pamphlets, articles and editorials in *Kudi Arasu* and *Viduthalai*. A lot of his works are still in print and many have even been digitized. His lack of formal education did not prevent him from expressing his views and thoughts on a wide range of subjects. His language is blunt and has none of the flowery alliteration that characterizes the works of other leaders of the Dravidian movement. As a publisher, he introduced reforms in the Tamil script to make it easier to print Tamil. Some of his changes were officially adopted to suit the Tamil typewriter keyboard layout in 1980 and are also used in Tamil fonts in computers. Periyar's ideology has inspired a whole generation of writers and artists in Tamil Nadu.

༼༽

Some of Periyar's ideals may seem ordinary now but one should remember that the world was a different place when Periyar first expressed and then lived by his ideals. Perhaps he is the only real iconoclast Tamil Nadu will ever see. Whether anyone agrees with his policies or not, no one can deny that Periyar's impact on Tamils and Tamil Nadu will continue to be felt for a long time.

Timeline

1879 (17 September) Birth of Periyar
1884 Temporarily adopted by a distant relative
1889 Withdrawn from school because of continuous mischief, back with his natural parents
1897 Courtship and marriage to Nagammal
1903 Runs away to Kashi
1910 Joins the Erode Municipal Council
1917 Joins the Madras Presidency Association (MPA)
1918 Becomes chairman of Erode Municipal Council; meets and becomes friends with Rajaji
1919 Joins the Indian National Congress at Rajaji's insistence. Resigns from all his government posts
1921 Participates in toddy shop boycott; cuts down 500 coconut trees in his own grove
1924 Participates in the Vaikom Satyagraha. Arrested and set free
1925 (2 May) launches the periodical *Kudi Arasu*
    (22 November) Leaves Congress
    (December) Launches Self-Respect Movement
1927 Supports the Simon Commission
    Implementation of the Communal G.O. of 1921

1928　Launches *Revolt*
1929　(February) First provincial conference of the Self-Respect Movement; drops 'Naicker' (caste suffix) from his name
1931　(13 December) Leaves on a tour of Russia, England and Europe
1932　(11 November) Returns from his foreign tour
　　　(28–29 December) Founds the Self-Respect and Equality Party
1933　(11 May) Death of his wife, Nagammal
　　　(December) Arrested for sedition
1934　(July) Communist Party of India banned; distances himself from Communists
　　　(November) Campaigns for Justice Party in council election. It loses the election
1937　(January) Campaigns for Justice Party in first assembly elections. It loses the election.
　　　(August) Rajaji announces compulsory Hindi in schools
　　　(December) Anti-Hindi coalition formed; unveils the 'Tamil Nadu for Tamils' slogan
1938　(April-November) Anti-Hindi agitation
　　　(November) Given the title Periyar (the great elder); arrested for inciting women to agitate
　　　(December) Elected as president of the Justice Party
1939　(May) Released from prison on health grounds
　　　(October) Rajaji government resigns
1940　(January) Meets B.R. Ambedkar and Muhammad Ali Jinnah at Bombay (February) Governor Erskine withdraws compulsory Hindi order; Dravida Nadu agitation; refuses offer to form a Justice government
1941　(August) Suspends Dravida Nadu agitation
1942　Campaign against Ramayana and Periyapuranam

1943 Appoints Maniammai as his personal aide
1944 (January) Salem conference; Justice Party becomes 'Dravidar Kazhagam'
1945 (September) Orders all party members to wear black shirts. First major clash with Anna.
1947 Orders party men to observe Independence Day as a day of mourning. Second major clash with Anna
1948 Anti-Hindi agitation again.
1949 (18 June) Marries Maniammai; Final clash with Anna (September) Anna leaves to form DMK
1950 Announces the Republic day as a day of mourning; Communal Rights agitation against Supreme Court order de-legitimizing reservations
1952 Supports Communist party in assembly elections; Rajaji becomes CM
1953 Kula Kalvi agitation and Pillaiyar idol breaking agitation
1954 Supports new Chief Minister Kamaraj in the Gudiyatham by-election
1956 Convinces Kamaraj to oppose Dakshin Pradesh proposal
1957 (March) Supports Congress in assembly elections; DMK contests elections for the first time
(June-December) Anti-Brahmin campaign
1958 Health declines; reduces public appearances
1959 Rajaji forms Swatantara Party
1962 Supports and campaigns for Congress again in assembly elections; Congress wins and DMK emerges the principal opposition.
1963 Kamaraj resigns as Chief Minister. Bhaktavatsalam succeeds him
1965 Does not support the second major anti-Hindi agitation and condemns the violence
1967 Supports and campaigns for Congress in assembly elections;

DMK wins and Anna becomes Chief Minister; reconciles with Anna
1969 Anna dies and Karunanidhi succeeds him as Chief Minister
1970 Temple sanctum entry agitation; withdraws agitation after Karunanidhi passes legislation to allow people of all castes to become priests
1971 Campaigns for DMK against Rajaji-Kamaraj coalition in assembly elections; DMK-Congress (I) wins
1972 Tries to mediate between Karunanidhi and MGR; condemns MGR when he starts a new party
1973 (24 December) Death

Endnotes

1. He mentions one such incident in an autobiographical essay. He once chased and caught a Brahmin debtor to produce him in court on behalf of a fellow merchant. The debtor tried to hide himself in a dining hall where a ritual feeding of two to three hundred Brahmins was taking place. Periyar went in through the roof and caught the debtor. But the Brahmins refused to touch the food saying his (a non-Brahmin's) presence had defiled the food. Other non-Brahmins, who had sponsored the feeding, complained to his father. Venkatar flew into a rage and beat him up in public for his 'inappropriate' behaviour.
2. War committee secretary, honorary recruiting officer, taluk board president, district board member, etc.
3. Hand-spun and hand-woven cloth manufactured by village artisans using a hand-spinning wheel.
4. Limited form of self-governance given to Indians by the Montagu-Chelmsford reforms. Important departments like Finance, Defence, Home, etc. remained under the control of the colonial governor and his executive council. Lightweight departments like sanitation, irrigation and education were

transferred to the cabinet of Indian members elected to the Legislative Council.
5. S. Satyamurthi (1887–1943)—Congress leader in Madras Presidency and rival of Rajaji. Was leader of the Congress faction that advocated cooperation with the British.
6. While most Tamil historians of the Dravidian movement exaggerate the role played by Periyar in the Vaikom struggle, Periyar's opponents generally try to dismiss his participation in the struggle. The truth lies somewhere in between. The agitation lasted from March 1924 to November 1925. Periyar was active in the movement during April and May 1924. He was imprisoned twice—first for a month and the next time for six months (he served only for four months). When he was released the second time, the Madras government arrested him for making treasonous speeches a year before. He seems to have played no role in the events of 1925. After the compromise was reached, he participated in the victory conference on 29 November 1925. The national Congress leadership and Gandhi wanted to keep the agitation an intra-Hindu and intra-Kerala affair. Periyar's followers claim that Gandhi deliberately kept Periyar's name out of the reports on the agitation in *Young India*.
7. The six party conferences were—Trichy (1919), Tirunelveli (1920), Thanjavur (1921), Tirupur (1922), Madurai (1923) and Thiruvannamalai (1924).
8. P. Subbarayan (1889–1962): A wealthy landlord and lawyer from Kumaramangalam, Salem district. At first he was with the Justice Party but later quit to become an independent politician. Though generally nationalistic in outlook, he did not have much in common with the Swarajists. He later joined the Congress in 1933.
9. The legal codes of ancient lawgiver Manu; considered as the

basis of Hindu society, they contain severe discriminatory clauses against women and lower castes.

10. By the 1950s, atheism became the official policy of the movement.
   Meetings began with members taking the oath that read:
   There is no God, there is no God, there is certainly no God... He who preaches God is a fool. He who propagates God is a criminal. He who worships God is a barbarian.

11. Periyar wanted reservation proportional to the percentage of population—a system in which non-Brahmins would have received a greater share of the spoils.

12. The First Communal GO (#613) was passed by the first Justice government in September 1921. It was implemented by the P. Subbarayan government by another GO (#1071) on 4 November 1927. Out of every 12 units (jobs or college seats) Brahmins were allotted 2; non-Brahmins 5; Anglo-Indians/Christians and Muslims 2 each, and Depressed classes (Harijans) got 1. In 1947, the interim government of independent India increased the allocations to Harijans (later scheduled castes) by one. By 1950, the allocations were done on the bases of units of 14. (non-Brahmins 6; Brahmins, Backward Hindus and Harijans 2 each; Christians and Muslims 1 each).

13. Edited by S. Ramanathan and Kuthoosi S. Gurusamy, it was published till 1931.

14. Ramamirtham and Periyar kept up the campaign over the next decade and half. In 1947, the practice was abolished by the Congress government.

15. W.P.A. Soundara Pandian Nadar (1893–1953) was an industrialist from Pattiveeranpatti in present-day Dindugal district. He was the president of the Nadar Maha Sangam and an influential community leader.

16. R.K. Shanmugam Chettiar (1892–1953) was an industrialist and later, the first finance minister of India.
17. A severe worldwide economic recession that lasted from 1929 till the early '40s.
18. Shapurji Saklatwala (1874–1976) was a Parsi communist leader from India, who had settled in Britain after marrying a British woman. He was a member of the Independent Labour Party and the British Parliament.
19. Sami Chidambaram (1900–1961), was one of the earliest followers of Periyar. He wrote Periyar's biography *Thamizhar Thalaivar* which remains the most referenced work on Periyar's early life.
20. The editorial in question was published on 29 October 1933 and contained phrases proscribed by the Criminal Law Amendment Act of 1932. It denounced the government as anti-poor and advocated its overthrow.
21. Ramakrishna Ranga Rao (1901–1978), the Raja of Bobbili, was the president of the Justice Party and chief minister of the Madras Presidency during 1932–37.
22. The Justice Party suffered from chronic intra-party squabbles. When the faction fight turned into open war at the party conference in October 1932, the Self-Respecters backed the Raja of Bobbili and his landlords' faction against the incumbent chief minister Munuswamy Naidu, whom they perceived as being closer to the Congress. Naidu was forced out as party president and later as chief minister. Raja of Bobbili became the new chief minister with the support of The Self-Respecter Party.
23. Section 124 of the Indian Penal Code deals with sedition.
24. P. Jeevanandam (1907–1963) was a communist leader from Kanyakumari district and a supporter of the Self-Respect Movement from 1926. When Periyar broke away from the

communists in 1934, he turned a bitter foe of Periyar. He later published a book titled 'Erode padhai sariya?' (Is the Erode way the correct one?), which was critical of Periyar and the Self-Respect Movement.
25. After the Communist Party of India was banned, the communist sympathizers within Congress regrouped and formed the Congress Socialist Party in 1934.
26. C.N. Annadurai (1909–1969): Founder of the Dravida Munetra Kazhagam (DMK) and the first non-Congress chief minister of Tamil Nadu. He was the strongest and by far the most ambitious of Periyar's lieutenants. He split from Periyar in 1949 to form the DMK party.
27. While ministries in other provinces were downsizing, Bobbili made an unsuccessful attempt to increase his cabinet size by one to accommodate all the factions within the party. The Justice ministers were paid more than double the salary of the ministers.
28. Under provincial autonomy, Indians were given more powers; all ministerial portfolios except Defence were transferred to the cabinet elected by Indians. The franchise was extended and about fifteen per cent of the total population became eligible to vote. The system also set up a bicameral legislature in the provinces replacing the old unicameral system under diarchy.
29. As early as 1918, Gandhi had formed the Dakshin Bharat Hindi Prachar Sabha (organization for propagating Hindi in South India). By 1925, Hindustani was being used for the official proceedings of the Congress. Apart from the Prachar Sabha, Hindustani Seva Dal and Hindustani Hitaishi Sabha were also involved in propagating Hindi/Hindustani in southern states.
30. Forms 1 to 6 were equivalents of the present day Class VI to XI.

31. A.T. Pannirselvam (1888–1940): Landlord from Thanjavur, Indian Christian leader and former Justice Party minister. One of the few Justicites to win in 1937 elections, he died in a plane crash in 1940.
32. Adherents of Shaivism, a major branch of Hinduism, and worshippers of Lord Shiva. Tamil Shaivites were also known for their devotion to the Tamil language. In the late 1920s and early 1930s, Shaivites and Self-Respecters involved in an acrimonious public feud. Through public conferences, speeches and journal articles, they routinely denounced each other's ideologies using harsh words.
33. Maraimalai Adigal (1876–1950): Shaivite Tamil scholar and proponent of the Thani Tamizh Iyakkam (Pure Tamil Movement); was a staunch opponent of Periyar till the anti-Hindi movement brought them together.
34. Pattukottai Azhagiri (1900–1949): A veteran activist of the Self-Respect Movement. He was nicknamed 'anja nenjan' (brave heart) for his unflinching belief in Periyar's ideology.
35. Sarvepalli Radhakrishnan (1888–1975): Philosopher and Congress leader; later became president of India.
36. Great Britain declared war on Germany in September 1939. India, as part of the British Empire was expected to follow suit. But the Indian National Congress did not want to get involved in a European war without obtaining independence first. But India's Viceroy Linlithgow unilaterally declared war on Germany without consulting them. Congress governments in eight Indian provinces resigned in protest.
37. Tamil, Telugu, Kannada and Malayalam.
38. Bow and arrow, tiger and fish were the respective emblems of Cheras, Cholas and Pandyas who ruled present day Tamil Nadu from about the 2nd century CE to the 13th century.
39. To secure Indian support in the Second World War, the British

sent a mission under Sir Stafford Cripps, a minister in the British war cabinet. Cripps promised increased autonomy and eventual independence for India in return for cooperation in the war. But the mission failed because of mutual distrust between the Congress and the British government.
40. A twelfth century Tamil epic written by poet Sekkizhar, it documents the lives of Shaivite poet-saints.
41. Nandanar—one of the sixty three Nayanmars (Shaivite saints). He belonged to the untouchable Parayar caste.
42. *Ramayana Paathirangal* (Characters of the Ramayana) first published in 1930 was more of a retelling than a character study. A detailed analysis of Periyar's views on Ramayana can be found in Paula Richman's *Many Ramayanas: The Diversity of a Narrative Tradition in South Asia*.
43. Periyar's version of the Ramayana was popularized by M.R. Radha in the form of the play named *Keemayanam* and the term came to be associated with Periyar.
44. P.T. Rajan (1892–1974) and A.P. Patro (1876–1946) were landlords from Madurai and Orissa respectively and former ministers in Justice governments; P. Balasubramaniam was the editor and publisher of the party magazine *Sunday Observer*; C.G. Netto was a lawyer from Salem and the Malayalee face of the party.
45. The party constitution did not specify any term limits for the party presidency. New presidents could be elected whenever the party's annual confederations were held. Presidents who wanted to hang on to the presidency avoided holding any confederations. Seven days before the scheduled sixteenth confederation, the dissidents met and passed a resolution saying any decision taken at the Salem confederation would not bind them.
46. B. Ramachandra Reddi (1894–1973): A long term Justice

legislator from Bezawada, Andhra Pradesh. As a Justice candidate he had won in all the previous elections except one.
47. It contested the 1952 elections as 'Justice Party' with 'scales' as its symbol. However, it soon lost its status as a recognized party but continued to exist as an unrecognized party till P.T. Rajan's death.
48. *Dravida Nadu* weekly owned and edited by Anna. It began publishing on 8 March 1942.
49. E.V.K. Sampath (1926–1971): Son of E.V. Krishnasamy, Periyar's elder brother. One of the founders of DMK along with Anna, he left DMK to form his own party in 1961 and later joined the Congress.
50. Black Shirts was also the name of an Italian fascist militia organized by the dictator Benito Mussolini.
51. Bharathidasan (1891–1964): Rationalist poet of the Dravidian movement. He used to be a nationalist but later became a supporter of Periyar.
52. Jamnalala Bajaj and Ghanshyam Das Birla: Industrialists and financial backers of the Indian National Congress.
53. M.R. Radha (1907–1979) was a stage and film actor and a follower of Periyar. He would later gain notoriety for shooting M.G. Ramachandran in 1971.
54. K.B. Sundarambal and M.S. Subbulakshmi were famous singers. Sundarambal was a known Congress supporter who campaigned for the party in elections.
55. Between 15 August 1947 when India got its independence, and 26 January 1950 when it became a republic, the Indian state was styled 'Dominion of India' with the British monarch as head of state and the governor general as his representative.
56. Section 75 of the Indian Penal Code dealt with punishment fo repeat offenders.

57. 'Fire will always burn and neem oil will always be bitter. They cannot shed their nature.' were his exact words. He was saying Anna was not trustworthy.
58. The three kinds of Tamil literature—Iyal (prose), Isai (music) and Nadagam (drama).
59. Those who wished to register a wedding had to issue a thirty day advance notice at the registrar's office and the bride and groom's details would be posted on the notice board.
60. A thinly veiled allusion to Hitler marrying his mistress Eva Braun, hours before he committed suicide.
61. It became a sort of unofficial list of the Anna faction. For years Periyar would use the term 'Kanneer Thuligal' derisively to refer to those who split from the party along with Anna.
62 State of Madras vs. Smt. Champakam Dorairajan (Supreme Court Case No 226, AIR 1951). Champakam Dorairajan petitioned against quotas in Madras Medical College (MMC) while C.R. Srinivasan petitioned against the College of Engineering, Guindy. It was later found that Champakam had filed a false affidavit as she had never applied for a seat in MMC.
63. The language question kept the Indian Constituent Assembly in a deadlock for a long time. A compromise called Munshi-Ayyangar formula was eventually worked out to satisfy all parties. The new republic would not have a national language; Hindi and English would be official languages and the latter would be phased out after fifteen years.
64. Prime Minister Nehru dismissed the tarring of Hindi boards as acts of 'childish nonsense' by 'immature people'.
65. In the republic of India, the Madras Presidency became the Madras State.
66. In the late 1940s, the CPI launched peasant rebellions in

Telengana, Bengal and the Tanjore and Malabar districts of the Madras State. The peasant revolts were crushed ruthlessly by the Congress governments at the state and the centre. After their defeat, the CPI announced its intention to participate in electoral politics.

67 'The Communists have their office at a foreign place like Bombay or Delhi', Periyar declared. 'They are only interested in exploiting us like the other foreign controlled parties. *Janasakthi*'s [CPI journal] editors are Brahmins and [as we know] wherever a Brahmin goes he is likely to support caste differences.' He also described the alliance as temporary.

68 Tanguturi Prakasam (1872–1953): Congress leader from Andhra. He was chief minister of the state during 1946–47 and leader of the Andhra faction of the Madras Congress. He quit Congress in 1951 and floated his own party—Kisan Mazdoor Praja Party.

69. Rajaji had been ousted as Union home minister in October 1951 and had retired from public life. When he was offered the post of the Indian high commissioner in the United Kingdom, he sarcastically wrote to Lord Mountbatten: 'My career is truly remarkable in its zigzag...cabinet minister, governor without power, governor general when the Constitution was to be wound up, minister without portfolio, home minister and... now the proposition is acting high commissioner in the UK! Finally, I must one day cheerfully accept a senior clerk's place somewhere and raise that job to its proper and honoured importance'.

70. He lured the Commonweal Party by offering a ministerial berth to its leader Manickavel Naicker; Ramasamy Padayachi followed Naicker; then Rajaji engineered a split in the Krishikar Lok Party and half its legislators joined the Congress. About a dozen independents, too, joined the Congress. The

Muslim League supported him to thwart the communists.
71. By law, the governor could nominate someone to the Council only if the cabinet recommended it. But in this case, there was no such recommendation, as there was no cabinet formed yet. Years later, the Sarkaria Commission, formed to analyse Centre-State relationships, would dub it as a 'constitutional impropriety'.
72. The official name for the scheme was 'Modified Scheme of Elementary Education'. It was variously referred to as 'Madras Elementary Education Scheme', 'New Education Scheme' and 'Madras Education Scheme' in the press. Rajaji's opponents dubbed it as Kula Kalvi Thittam and Acharyar Kalvi Thittam.
73. Part of a three-pronged agitation; other two prongs for renaming Dalmiapuram as Kallakudi and condemning Nehru for calling DMK's actions 'childish nonsense'.
74. C.N. Annadurai, E.V.K. Sampath, N.V. Natarajan, K.A. Mathiazhagan and V.R. Nedunchezhiyan.
75. K. Kamaraj (1903–1975): Chief minister of Tamil Nadu between 13 April 1954–2 October 1963. He was elected thrice to the post of chief minister. In 1952, he was the leader of the Tamil Nadu Congress and chief rival of Rajaji within the party.
76. Periyar did not consider Brahmins Tamils; hence Rajaji was not counted as a Tamil CM. All other previous chief ministers had been Telugus. His preferred term for Kamaraj was Pachai Tamizhan (the Real Tamil).
77. While the Dravida Nadu included Andhra and Rayalseema areas, the proposal for Dakshina Pradesh did not include them. It included present day Tamil Nadu, Malabar district, parts of South Canara district and the princely states of Cochin and Travancore.
78. Though there was an internal referendum, party leaders

including Anna made it clear that they wanted to contest elections.
79. Periyar had first raised the 'Brahmin hotel' issue in 1940.
80. Periyar usually used colourful epithets to describe his opponents. For him, Anna and DMK were always kanneer thuligal (teardrops) as they had once described themselves while mourning Periyar's decision to marry Maniammai. And for Rajaji's Swatantara party Periyar's chosen term was Kalla nottu gumbal (fake currency party)—a potshot at Rajaji's conservative economic policies.
81. Food production using traditional agricultural methods was not able to keep up with the population growth. The government launched the 'Green Revolution' to radically revamp agriculture and increase food production. As a temporary measure, it accepted food aid from the United States under the PL-480 scheme. But it was too late to save the Congress government in Madras.
82. It was a rainbow coalition comprising CPI, DMK, Swatantara and a number of smaller parties like M.P. Sivagnanam's Tamil Arasu Kazhagam and S.B. Adithan's Naam Thamizhar. Despite contradictory ideological backgrounds, they had a single common agenda–ousting the Congress.
83. It was an enormously popular election promise in a state wracked with food shortage. DMK announced that it would provide three padis (measures) of rice for one rupee and declared if they failed to do so, the people can 'whip them' in public. Anna couldn't keep his promise. The scheme was implemented only in a few areas of Madras and later abandoned completely.
84. The party did not have a president as long as Anna was alive. The general secretary was the party leader. After Anna's death, the president's post was created as part of the Karunanidhi–

Nedunchezhiyan compromise and Karunanidhi became the president. Since then, the general secretary remains a figurehead in the party.

85. Brahmin and other caste hereditary priests' associations went to court against the legislation. After several contradictory verdicts in various courts, the scheme was finally implemented by a Government Order in 2006. But in 2009 the Supreme Court stayed the government's efforts to appoint non-Brahmin priests and the future of the scheme is not clear.
86. The Indira faction was led by Prime Minister Indira Gandhi, while the Organization Congress was led by the Syndicate—a group of older Congress leaders like Morarji Desai and Kamaraj.
87. At a superstition eradication conference in 1971, party volunteers garlanded and hit Lord Ram's pictures with slippers.
88. MGR's opponents in the DMK alleged that he had problems with the income tax department and was pressured by Indira Gandhi to split the party in return for the central government going easy on him.

References

I. Anandhi, S. 'Women's Question in the Dravidian Movement c. 1925–1948'. *Social Scientist* vol.19, nos 5-6., 1991.

II. Arnold, David. *The Congress in Tamilnad: Nationalist Politics in South India, 1919–1937*. New Delhi: Manohar Publications, 1977.

III. Austin, Granville. *The Indian Constitution: Cornerstone of a Nation*. New Delhi: Oxford University Press, 1999.

IV. Hodges, Sarah. *Contraception, Colonialism and Commerce: Birth Control in South India, 1920–1940*. United Kingdom: Ashgate Publishing, 2008.

V. Gandhi, Rajmohan. *The Rajaji Story*. Mumbai: Bharatiya Vidya Bhavan, 1984.

VI. Irschick, Eugene F. *Tamil Revivalism in the 1930s*. Chennai: Cre-A, 1986.

VII. ―――― *Political and Social Conflict in South India: The Non-Brahmin Movement and Tamil Separatism, 1916–1929*. Berkeley: University of California Press, 1969.

VIII. Jeevanandam, P Erodu Paadhai Sariya?

IX. Kandaswamy, W.B. Vasantha, Florentin Smarandache and

	K. Kandasamy. *Fuzzy and Neutrosophic Analysis of Periyar's Views on Untouchability*, USA: American Research Press, 2005.
X.	Kannan, R. *Anna: The Life and Times of C.N. Annadurai.* New Delhi: Penguin Books, 2010.
XI.	Karunanandham. *Kavignar Thanthai Periyar Vaazhkai Varlaaru,* Thamizk Kudiyarasu Pathippagam, 1979.
XII.	*Malarmannan Thimuka thondriyadhu yen?* Kizhakku Pathippagam, 2009.
XIII.	Manikumar, K.A. *A Colonial Economy in the Great Depression, Madras (1929-1937).* Hyderabad: Orient Blackswan, 2003.
XIV.	More, J.B. Prashant. *The Political Evolution of Muslims in Tamilnadu and Madras, 1930-1947.* Hyderabad: Orient Longman, 1997.
XV.	Muthukumar, R. *Periyar.* Kizhakku Pathippagam, 2008.
XVI.	Pandian M. S. S., S. Anandhi and A.R. Venkatachalapathi. 'Of Maltova Mothers and Other Stories'. Economic and Political Weekly. Vol.26. nos. 16, 1991.
XVII.	Parthasarathi, T.M. *Hi Mu Ka Varalaaru.* Bharathi Pathippakam, 1961.
XVIII.	Rajaraman, P. *The Justice Party: A Historical Perspective, 1916-37.* Chennai: Poompozhil Publishers, 1988.
XIX.	Ramanathan, K.V. *The Satyamurti Letters: The Indian Freedom Struggle Through the Eyes of a Parliamentarian, Volume 1.* New Delhi: Pearson Education India, 2008.
XX.	Ramasamy, E.V. *Periyarin Thanvaralaaru Periyar Dravida Kazhagam,* 2007.
XXI.	Ramaswamy, Sumathy. *Passions of the Tongue: Language Devotion in Tamil India, 1891-1970.* Berkeley: University of California Press, 1997.
XXII.	Ravichandran, R. 'Dravidar Kazhagam: A Political Study.' Madras University unpublished thesis, 1982.

XXIII. Richman, Paula, Ed. *Many Ramayanas: The Diversity of a Narrative Tradition in South Asia*. Berkeley: University of California Press, 1991.
XXIV. Sami Chidambaram. *Thamilar Thalaivar, Periyar Suya Mariyadhai Prachara Veliyeedu*, 2001.
XXV. Sivalai Ilamathi Thimukavin Thorramum Valarchiyum Manimekalai Prasuram, 1997.
XXVI. Sundararajan, Saroja. *March to Freedom in Madras Presidency, 1916–1947*. Chennai: Lalitha Publications, 1989.
XXVII. Thirunavukkarasu Ka. *Dravida Iyakka Thoongal*. Nakkeran Padippagam, 1999.
XXVIII. Venkatachalapathy, A.R. *In Those Days There was No Coffee: Writings in Cultural History*. New Delhi: Yoda Press, 2006.
XXVIII. Venu, A.S. *Verdict on Verdict*. Kalai Mandram, 1953.

Online Resources
- http: //www.periyardk.org
- http: //tamizachi.com
- http: //tamilhindu.com
- http: //www.periyarevr.org

www.ingramcontent.com/pod-product-compliance
Lightning Source LLC
Chambersburg PA
CBHW032003080426
42735CB00007B/493